The Teacher's Teacher

Mark Mainella

Published by Mainline Publishing
41 Colonial Avenue · Barrington, RI 02806
Tel.: 401-245-1847 · Fax: 401-245-3534
E-mail: mark@mainellaseminars.com

ISBN: 978-0-578-03046-3

This book is dedicated to my family:
Joan, Mark, Katy, Kristina, Doug, Julia, Gracie, Luis and
Vincent.

You made a difference.

Joan, thank you for telling me what I need to hear, not what I want to hear. You have been my strongest supporter and most severe critic for 50 years.

About the Starfish . . .

Based on the writing of Loren Eiseley in "The Star Thrower" The story was first told to me by John Dzerkacz, one of my strongest supporters in the academic community. I completed a presentation at his school, Montachusett Regional Vocational Technical High School. At the conclusion, he presented me with a starfish pin and said "Mark, you made a difference today." I had no idea about the symbolism of the starfish. I later learned the story of the starfish and began closing my seminars with it. The story goes *something* like this:

A man was jogging along the beach after a major storm had just come through the area. The huge number of starfish that the storm had washed up on the beach dismayed him. He thought there was nothing he could do because of the immense numbers. As he continued along the beach, he saw a little boy in the distance throw something into the water. As he got closer, he saw the boy walk a little further down the beach, bend over, pick up a starfish and throw it into the water. As the jogger approached, the boy stopped again bent over, picked up another starfish and was about to throw it in the water. The jogger stopped and asked, "Why are you doing that? There are thousands of starfish on the beach. You can't possibly make a difference." The little boy looked at the starfish, threw it into the water and replied, "I made a difference to that one, didn't I?"

I now give a gold starfish pin to anyone I encounter that tries to make a difference in someone's life. I couldn't but for the generosity of Peter Wallach, CEO of Tanya Creation's Inc. I was at a wedding at the Viking Hotel in Newport, RI where I met Peter. He asked why I was wearing the starfish pin on my lapel and I explained I was an inspirational speaker. I told him the story and he loved it. He asked if I gave them out to the people I meet that make a difference and I said no, I can't afford to. Peter said, "Now you can, my company will supply them." I asked why and he said, "great teachers made a difference in my life and I would like to help."

Special thanks to Peter Wallach; Tanya Creations, Inc.

The Teacher's Teacher

August 30, 1916 - July 7, 2003

Nancy Stevenson was a nationally known special educator. She was the author of *The Natural Way to Reading* and founder of the Stevenson Language Skills Program. Mrs. Stevenson was an innovator who developed teaching methods for both regular and learning disabled students. Mrs. Stevenson's critique of *The Teacher's Teacher* can be summarized with the following:

"Every teacher in America should have this book on their desk for reference purposes."

Special thanks to Cam Stevenson for his friendship, support as well as presenting my book to his Mother for review.

Duffy, Schoonmacher, Gassaway, Cavalaro, Sargalski, Artuso, Bagnigni, Montamuro, and Mainella

About the Gassaway Tour

I invited some of the top administrators to visit Boys and Girls high school, 1700 Fulton Street in Brooklyn, NY. I wanted them to witness, firsthand, the great leadership of Principal Bernard Gassaway in this very difficult environment. The walk through of the school resulted with each member of the visiting team being blown away by the attitude, the expectations, and the commitment of Bernard and his team.

The bottom line realization was simple; when students, any student, from any environment, know that people care, they respond accordingly.

After the visit we went to see Joe Artuso at his bakery on 187th street in the Bronx. He took us on an insider's tour of Arthur Avenue and we finished the day having lunch at Tino's Deli. The camaraderie, the learning experience, the relationships that have been established over the years made for an absolutely fabulous day.

Table of Contents

Foreword

Life is a series of ups and downs. It is a time that is short, and filled with promises that are often broken. Many people spend a lifetime searching for direction in an attempt to find happiness.

One of the most important ingredients in finding fulfillment and happiness in our lives is a positive self-image, and this image is often the product of the messages we send to ourselves. If our attitude and self-concept are positive, we usually act accordingly. When the reverse is true, that image is like a vulture shadowing us, sucking away at what is good. We learn to depend upon the validation of others, rather than seeking our own.

Youth is a time of great turbulence as people try to gain their true identity. Too often, they are told they are bad and worthless. They have doubts about who they are and where they are headed. Many give up. Educators therefore face a tremendous challenge. We need to consider the whole student; every student, all the time. Above all, we need to show students that we care.

Mark Mainella's work with both students and teachers is unique. Mark has that special quality that makes an audience really listen and understand that they are important. He eloquently shares his own life of doubts and put-downs and how he finally rose above negativity. His message is one of hope and inspiration: to believe in oneself. Mark promotes a positive attitude and an overwhelming commitment to pursuing one's maximum potential.

I have been privileged many times to see the magical spell Mark casts upon his audience. He offers people honesty and the knowledge that we are in charge of our own destiny. Mark's words have helped countless people recommit to the excellence that they are capable of achieving — and that is the focus of this outstanding book. *The Teacher's Teacher* is an experience not to be missed.

Dr. Justus D. Anderson
Director of Guidance, Seekonk High School (retired)

Introduction

Most of us don't realize that, next to our parents, teachers are probably the most influential people in our lives, for good and for ill. This was certainly true in my case. I had a teacher in elementary school that was rude, crude and extremely insensitive. She was nasty to me and regularly suggested to me and to my classmates that I was not going to succeed at the game of life. In fact, she made me believe that I wouldn't live very long. She was a poor excuse for a human being, let alone for a teacher, and the damage she inflicted took years to repair.

But I have also been touched in my life by some great teachers. I call them the Teacher's Teachers: the ones who set an example for other teachers to follow and learn from. This book is about them — not about the wrong that is done in education but about the greatness I have seen. I want to talk about how to maximize the individual's potential for learning — every individual, whatever his or her inherent skill level, ethnic, racial, or religious background, or socioeconomic circumstances. To this end I would like to share with you what I have learned over the past 33 plus years, traveling this country, speaking in approximately 200 high schools per year, lecturing on college campuses and prisons, conducting in-service seminars for faculty and working in the private sector. I have talked with, listened to, and learned from students, teachers, administrators and people in business; and from this vast base of knowledge I have assembled the ideas presented in this book.

We are constantly reading, hearing and being told that American schools aren't doing their job, that other countries' students outperform ours, and that U.S. students have inferior test scores. The simple truth is, though, that we approach education very differently from other countries. In Japan and

Germany, for example, students are tested at an early age (twelve or thirteen years old), and only those who demonstrate a certain level of academic proficiency are allowed to go on to finish high school. On the other hand, in America we give all students the opportunity to complete their secondary education. We're willing to invest our time and resources toward helping all our students—even those who don't meet a standardized set of very limited criteria. In other words, we recognize that not all children will perform well on a written examination, and yet we give them an equal opportunity to prove that they can still be a respected, productive member of our society. We give the same opportunity to all of our children, wherever their strengths may exist. This is just one of many wonderful facets of our strong, just and tremendously valuable system of education.

So this book is about winning our students, not losing them. It's about strategies, techniques, approaches, and the near-magic that the great teachers have taught me. The letters following each chapter testify to the strength and caring that are all around us, and the huge impact we can have on the lives of students. I hope you will find it helpful in your pursuit of excellence in the classroom, in the workforce and in your day-to-day living. There is no greater satisfaction than in knowing that your efforts, your caring, your giving, your listening, your sharing, and your commitment to helping the individual grow and pursue greater knowledge have been successful — and there is no greater goal than to wake up every morning and commit to excellence. Through your commitment to ongoing learning, the story of the Teacher's Teacher will continue.

Mark Mainella

Chapter 1

Facing the Challenge

We've all had them, one that we hated and one that we loved. One who was really sharp, another who bored us to tears. One who was cool, another who was a real jerk. Even now we all have one that we'll never forget, good or bad, while many have been long since forgotten. Yes, we're talking about teachers. We're talking about the people who, second only to our parents, were probably the most powerful influence in our entire lives.

As a teacher, you face amazing challenges every day. You don't have the luxury of a "comfort zone," of going to the office on almost any day and knowing exactly what to expect. Unlike most people in the career and business world, you can't even assume that most of the people you deal with have chosen to be there. You know that you're the constant subject of scrutiny, criticism, humor and gossip. You certainly know that your efforts are not paid anything close to what they're worth. And yet, the odds are that *you love what you do*. In that simple fact you're very fortunate, since it's something that 75% of working adults can't claim. Statistics tell us that three out of four Americans hate their jobs! It says something about you that — despite those numbers and despite having one of the most difficult jobs our society has created — you find your job to be immensely rewarding.

What are the specific challenges you face? These are troubled times, as the media tells us every day. The ideal learning situation rarely exists, and the different schools and educational environments are as varied as the many people within them.

Each has its own culture, with its special strengths and its special problems, any one of which can make your already monumental task even more difficult. Yet you have chosen to dedicate yourself to giving the best of yourself to your students, and to helping them realize the best in themselves, whatever that may take — and all of our society owes you its thanks.

My purpose in this book is to help you accomplish that goal, first by helping you to see what is wonderful about you and about the teaching profession, and then by sharing with you some of the things my travels over the years have taught me about America's finest teachers. Among our teachers there are some very special people whom I call the Teacher's Teacher — that is, the best of the best, the ones who can teach the rest of us — and you can become one, if you haven't already. The Teacher's Teacher loves people. He or she is a giver, and a person who cares. He or she is committed to using positive reaffirmation to help each and every student feel good and achieve his or her maximum potential. Most of all, the Teacher's Teacher understands the true measure of success.

There are many roadblocks on the way to becoming the Teacher's Teacher. There will be many successes, and there will be some failures, both big and small. But you can get there by remaining committed to your goals. You can get there by losing the fear and being ready to live your dream.

In the Beginning, There Was Fear

Think back to the first time you walked into your students' classroom. Were you nervous? Awkward? Even petrified? Of course, the first day at any job can be unnerving, but your first day as a teacher is even more so because *you've been where your students are*. You're looking at yourself through their eyes, filtered through the screen of your own memories, both good and bad. What do you see? You see all the things you know can go wrong, because you've already seen them happen — you've been therebefore. With luck you also see all the great things you want to do, the examples of great teachers you've had yourself, the high standard they set. And along with the inspiration these examples bring, they may also carry the anxiety that you won't be able to meet the challenge.

How do you cope with fear when things go wrong? How do you keep yourself committed and confident in the face of possible failure? This is one of the biggest challenges we all face, and our impulse may be to try to avoid failure at all costs — by setting impossibly high standards, by anxious over preparation, by putting pressure on ourselves and others. But does this really help? When things do go wrong — and they will, despite our best efforts — we need a way of handling that failure and moving on.

Once at an in-service at a high school, a teacher stood up, made a rude gesture and walked out. She had been in the front row and no one saw it, so I continued with my presentation rather than disrupt the session. Then, when she was at the back of the auditorium and everybody had turned, she repeated the rude gesture. The entire incident was bizarre; I couldn't think of anything I had done that could have offended her. I truly love my work with all the students and teachers, but even in the most wonderful of careers the best of intentions occasionally backfire. Clearly despite my best efforts, I hadn't connected with this teacher.

In cases like this, we've got to acknowledge our right to fail. Regardless of whether we're the ones responsible (and very often we aren't), situations and efforts can go awry. This is an essential fact of life. It's very important at times like these to be able to put these failures in perspective. We — and those who love and support us — must look at these situations as part of the inevitable law of averages. The question to ask here is "what happened?" and not necessarily "what did I do wrong?" If we're not at fault, we need to be at peace with that fact and not keep replaying the scene in our heads, endlessly wondering why.

Of course, there will be times when we must accept that we did something wrong. For teachers, this may be something as simple as letting our energy level drop, or failing to look or listen at one crucial time, or letting our personal problems set up a smokescreen between us and our students. This will happen, and sometimes harm will result. But that harm is rarely irreparable, and the student we neglected to connect with today will be far less hurt if we reconnect with him tomorrow than if we appear to have brushed him off altogether. When we realize we've failed, the next question to ask is "how can I make things better?" It's never "how can I punish myself?" or "how long should I dwell on this issue?" We've got to give ourselves permission to fail, and then to turn that failure into just a small marker on our path to success — by learning from a mistake, by gaining insight into ourselves and others. Our students are what's important here, not our own self-assessments. And we need to keep our eyes on what's important.

Attitude is the key to recovery when things go terribly wrong. When most people recall what they perceive as their worst failures, often their most vivid recollections have to do with humiliation rather than errors committed. For the human psyche, a humiliating experience can seem to leave wounds that will never heal, and those memories constantly plague and haunt us, unless we expend vast amounts of energy to keep shoving them back beneath the surface. Educators are particularly vulnerable here, since criticism and satire for us are a way of life. Students do enjoy a good laugh at our expense; that's an occupational hazard we have to endure. We are always in the public view, and none of us will always be seen at our best. But just as we can show our students that it's okay to fail occasionally, we need to show them that attitude and perseverance can overcome even the most ego-wrenching debacle.

Success means having a *balance* whereby we can have a history and not feel ashamed. There's no reason to dwell on guilt or blame or humiliation. Our own attitudes will set the limits and will help us keep the focus on our goals.

Getting Beyond the Fear

As teachers, we hold tremendous power; and that power comes with a tremendous responsibility. In the past, that power was often exercised in more obvious ways — for instance, it was socially acceptable to use physical threats and humiliation, such as slapping the knuckles with a ruler or using the "dunce cap" to scare and shame students into compliance. Rewards, on the other hand, often hid a tacit criticism of one student in excessive praise for another one, thus creating an unfair system of *comparing children* in a battle that they knew they could not win. In recent years we have finally come to admit that much of what we once called "reinforcement" was not only destructive and demeaning but also contrary to the entire purpose of education. Today parents and teachers know that one of the most essential components of successful learning is mutual respect.

We've certainly come a long way! But our responsibilities have not changed. We can never afford to underestimate the far-reaching effects of our influence, and this very knowledge can be a powerful source of fear. There are also many other types of fear that can be holding us back. There is the fear of change, and the fear of the new. There is always the fear of failure and in many cases even the fear of success. We may occasionally doubt our level of commitment, or worry about external circumstances that can change the outcome. We may be afraid of how we measure up to our strongest critics: ourselves.

The memory of our own experience as students can be a powerful force. Whether your school experiences were positive or negative, the teacher that you are has largely been shaped by the student that you were, and by the teachers who influenced you. A great teacher in your own past can be an important source of inspiration. And if you had a negative experience, you may resolve to right the wrongs and prevent similar damage.

Many people go into teaching primarily for these reasons, and they are fine as far as they go. But you need more than this to help you deal with the responsibility and risk of teaching and the fear that comes with it. This is the central question I want to address: how can we take these risks and responsibilities and make them into opportunities for success, rather than crippling sources of anxiety that keep us from achieving our ideals?

This book is about success in its truest sense, both for us and for our students. For adults, success consists of finding something that we love doing and then committing to an ongoing excellence in doing it. Nowhere is this truer than in the teaching profession! For our students, we need to help them understand — and show them that we understand — that true success in life can't be measured by test scores. True success is having a positive sense of self and a commitment to ongoing self-improvement. When we lose our fear, or learn to move beyond it, then we can start to teach, and live, to our fullest potential.

Chapter 2

Travels Through Time

Today's teacher stands at the end of a long line of educators dating back to ancient times. We also stand at the beginning of the line for the students we influence today and the teachers who follow us tomorrow. Understanding where we have come from as a profession and how our American educational system works can give us a good perspective on our important place in history. How did we get here? You may be surprised.

The Early Years

Of course formal education didn't originate in the United States — we borrowed our ideas about education from other cultures. Plato advocated education as a way of developing good citizens for Greece. A fellow philosopher, Socrates, is thought of as one of the first to teach critical thinking skills. Later the Romans expanded on the ideas of the Greeks by teaching their boys to read, write and count. Upper-class Romans could continue their education by learning Latin grammar and literature. During the Middle Ages, education fell far behind the ideals of Greece and Rome. There was a long period of illiteracy that lasted until the Renaissance, when wealthy European children once again found themselves immersed in learning.

The early settlers of Colonial America brought their ideas about education with them from Europe. Affluent families sent their children to private schools or hired tutors. Poorer families could neither afford the expense of sending their children to school nor the loss of their help on the farm. These children of the lower class learned through apprenticeship, if they were lucky. Many had no schooling at all.

The trend toward universal education was first promoted by Protestant religious leaders, who wanted young people to be able to learn and interpret the Bible. In 1635, American education took a major stride toward this goal with the founding of the Public Latin School of Boston. The movement spread throughout the country with the passing of the Old Deluder Satan Act in 1647, requiring every township of 50 or more families to provide a teacher to instruct children in reading and writing. The act also called for towns of 100 or more families to pay for a secondary school to prepare young men for college. The major motivation for passing the act was to thwart that "old deluder," Satan. Schools fell into step with this mission by instilling in each student a moral code as well as knowledge of the Latin and Greek classics. Harvard College, the first university in the United States, was founded to train Latin School graduates for the ministry. It was not until the passage of the First Amendment, which separated church and state at least nominally, that religion stopped being the primary focus of education.

Americans embraced the idea of educating the masses, while our European counterparts believed that ability is limited and only those who possess it should attend school. Early U.S. education policies echoed the philosophy of Horace Mann, the first secretary of education in Massachusetts, who said, "The scientific or literary well-being of a community is to be estimated not so much by its possessing a few men [sic] of great knowledge as its having many men of competent knowledge." Have we come as far from this as it might seem at first glance?

Education for all children, rich and poor, was certainly a positive step in our history. Besides teaching the three Rs, early schools also taught morality and patriotism, two excellent subjects indeed. The methods of instilling such knowledge, however, often left a lot to be desired. Our romantic notion of the one-room schoolhouse of "simpler times" is very far from the truth. Students in colonial times had to endure frigid cold in the winters and oppressive heat in the summers. Their lessons were drilled in through memorization rather than teaching them to think for themselves. And the threat of physical punishment always hung in the air.

Reaching Out

Although it clearly had its faults, our system of education benefited the many European immigrants who came to this country in the 19th and 20th centuries. In addition to teaching English to the newest members of our society, educators also introduced them to the American way of life. Regardless of economic status, ethnic background or religion, all children were entitled to a public school education — and with it the gift of equal opportunity and upward mobility in American society. At least that was the theory as it was expounded.

Unfortunately, the 19th-century founders of the common school were not nearly as sensitive to the needs of some of those people. It took over 100 years before the idea of "separate but equal" schools was abolished by the 1954 landmark case of Brown versus the Board of Education. Only then could Native and African Americans begin their long journey toward true freedom — a struggle that continues to this day.

Education for young women also evolved dramatically. My mother graduated from the eighth grade in the late 1920s and had a graduation ceremony far more lavish than most high school graduation ceremonies today. Why? Because that was the end of her education. As late as the 1940s very few women went on to high school. At age 14, girls went to work. While the 1950s brought a definite improvement, they were still the Dark Ages for women — a girl was told either she could become a secretary and work for men, or she could teach (and probably work for men). My sister-in-law, who is a very bright person, was told by her (female) English teacher in her senior year, "Why would you even consider taking college preparatory courses? You're going to be a secretary. That's it. That is what you can expect." When you're told something often enough, you tend to believe it, and young women were told that all the time.

Understand, though, that our modern perspective on secretaries may create a misleading angle on this story. There was a time when a female working as a secretary was considered revolutionary. Until the turn of the century, there was no such thing as a woman secretary in the business world. Men operated the typewriters, a new invention at the time. It was Katherine Gibbs who popularized the opportunity for college-educated women to do something other than teach. She started her school with about half a dozen women, trained them in secretarial skills and taught them how to "behave" in an office. She had firm standards — white gloves, hair styled in a bun, severe business attire — and created the "Gibbs Woman." These women secretaries earned about half of what men earned doing the same job.

Encouraging women to pursue their dreams was a gradual process. Even in the seventies, while girls were told they could do anything they wanted, they were discouraged from dreaming big. For example, they might have been told, "You can study anything you want, but people will never bring their animals to a woman veterinarian", or their legal problems to a woman lawyer or their aircraft design to a woman engineer. Fortunately for all of us, at some point girls stopped tolerating this. As I travel to schools these days I never hear young women say, "I can't do it because I am a woman." What I hear them saying instead, and it is very satisfying to me, is "I can do anything I want." And because of the trend-setting women who have come before them, I know they're right.

So by 1970, everyone had an equal opportunity, at least according to the law, right? Wrong! One of the last (and most frequently overlooked) classifications of student rights wasn't addressed until 1974 with the Education for All Handicapped

Children Act. This law first guaranteed all handicapped grade school students a proper education. Under this law, many disabled children actually went to school for the first time. Many others were mainstreamed — that is, taken out of special classes and mixed with the regular students. Unfortunately, though, they still faced massive barriers when they got *out* of school, as businesses showed wide-scale unwillingness to spend money to accommodate their needs.

Most changes in that regard didn't even *begin* until 1990 when the Americans with Disabilities Act was signed into law, forcing corporate America to open its doors.

Is the struggle over? Hardly. Even now, gay and lesbian students and adults are fighting for their rights. After them will come others. With every battle won, a new one begins. It's not that these issues are new — it's that some are only beginning to be recognized, and some won't even dawn on us for decades to come. The quest for true equality never ends. This is one sad but inevitable lesson we must teach our students. But we must also teach them that good things will result, and that they can play a major part in this wonderful evolution.

Education in a New Age

Although it remains far from perfect, formal education has made great strides since the beginning of our history. It can be uplifting to focus on how far we have come instead of always dwelling on how far we have yet to go. Consider that only 100 years ago, less than 10% of the nation's 14 to 17 year olds graduated from high school. By 1950, that figure rose to 34%. In 1985, 74% of that same age group were receiving their diplomas. So, you can see that, for all of our faults and scrutiny from a dissatisfied public, our school system has moved steadily toward meeting its goal of providing an education to every child.

Our schools have also accepted the challenge of adapting to changing times. As the needs of the work world have changed, so have the courses offered. In addition to teaching the classics, English grammar and history, schools began to offer a smorgasbord of courses ranging from keyboarding skills to driver education to physics. The new curriculum has required us to stretch our capabilities even further. Besides the challenge of educating everyone, we must now teach them more than ever before. This is a need that will certainly not go away in our current information age.

We expect a lot from our schools, *and yet we are told every day by the media how unsatisfied we are with them.* I believe we have to do more work to arrive at the real truth about our schools' performance. There are some tough questions that can give us a better handle on reality. Are schools achieving their goal of providing an equal education for all? Are students ready for the workforce when they leave our schools? Should it be left entirely to the school system to fully prepare them, or should families and businesses be doing more?

There are many reports lately showing how the American system of education compares to the educational processes of other developed countries. It is important that we carefully analyze the facts underlying these statistics. While we must be open to learning from their strengths, test score comparisons are often far too simplistic to be meaningful. In many European systems, for example, the students are tested at 16 and only those who pass the test go on to college. Naturally, the test scores of those who remain will be higher than the cumulative total of American graduates because we encourage *everyone* to complete their education, regardless of their ability to perform well on tests. Do you see how easily the statistics can be misunderstood? We have nothing to be ashamed of, and everything to be proud of here.

We also need to be conscious of our knee-jerk reaction of telling students that the best thing for them is to complete their education at a college or university. Ever since World War II and the G.I. Bill, we have bought into the belief that a college education is the best springboard into the working world.

However, today nearly half of the students with a four-year college degree do not find a career-related position within one year after graduation. College, as we have come to think of it, is not the only answer.

What business needs, and therefore what the younger generation needs, are specific skills. For every high-level position that exists for an electrical engineer, there are many more positions for hands-on electronics technicians who attended a vocational school and trained for real-world jobs. Likewise, there are many more jobs for people who fix computers than for those who design them.

What does this mean for us as educators of today's and tomorrow's job seekers? It means we should listen carefully to the high school students who say they do not want to go to college. Guide them toward learning about the other options. Let them know about the education offerings where hands-on skills are a priority. The degree they end up with may be less glamorous, but far more practical for them. Finding something they like to do will bring them more happiness and perhaps even substantial financial success. Consider that some plumbers make more than some doctors these days. If they choose the hands-on route and find they miss the balance of a more traditional four-year college education, they can always go back to school in the evenings to learn about art or the classics or whatever personal enrichment courses delight their minds.

Encourage your students to be honest about what they really want to do with their lives. Those who choose college only because they think it is expected of them are living a lie that could take decades — or longer — to undo. *By connecting to each individual*, you can help your students to sort through the maze of options and expectations that burden their decisions. As the teacher who helps to make things clearer for them, you will have a very important role in their own personal history — and in the continuing evolution of education in America.

Chapter 3

The Teacher's Teacher

Don Pastine, principal of Central High School in Providence, RI, was lambasted in the newspaper about Central's low-test scores. He said to me, "Mark, it's a joke how the media presents us — *their* take on how we're supposedly failing." I could not have agreed more, and here are some of the reasons why. For instance, I rarely see anyone mention that up until the age of 12, more than half of the 2000 students at Central were educated overseas, in countries such as Ecuador, Cambodia and Haiti. Many of these students come to us with only a marginal command of English. What's more, in reviewing some of Central High School's paperwork, I observed that over 500 *new* students came into the building during one month, and close to that number left it. These are not attrition or dropout statistics. This is the nature of a *transitional population*, where one quarter of the student body actually *came and went* in the first two months.

How would some of our suburban schools even attempt to deal with something like this? And do the media honestly expect schools like Central to present test scores comparable to those of the suburban high school kids who have been in the system for 12 consecutive years? It boggles the mind. Yet the fact is that these transplanted students do succeed. They graduate and go on to colleges, trade schools, and meaningful careers. These students are not daunted by the scare stories and half-truths about our educational system and neither are we. We know better. We've seen the proof in action, hundreds and thousands of times. I can only say that the Central High Schools across the country are doing *fabulously*, considering the circumstances. The Teacher's Teachers are showing that they have a singular commitment to helping *all* students, including those going in and out the revolving door. After all, isn't life a revolving door also? We can go in, out, or through it, but we'll get nowhere walking away from it.

Where do these teachers direct their efforts? The answer may surprise you. Many students will succeed with or without our help. They have the drive, the capability and the support. Others can only succeed with our help — they succeed *because of* our help. We need to make sure that they have it. It's the student that doesn't have the support system, doesn't have the drive, and doesn't have the commitment who needs the best teachers the most. These are the ones for whom we became teachers. When we focus our efforts on these students, the rewards are immeasurable. And the best teachers, in my opinion, are the ones who are most sensitive to and who recognize that inevitable truth. They are the ones who will give whatever disproportionate amount of time is necessary to the neediest rather than the most receptive.

It's true that there is some correlation between test scores and home situations involving supportive families. I visited a rural community in the middle of New York state where there were a lot of problems with test scores because most of the students come from households where education isn't a priority, or even held in much esteem. If the student doesn't come to school in a learning mode, then the teacher finds it very difficult to overcome this "hey, I don't care — education doesn't mean anything" attitude that is reinforced by the parents. This is a far greater challenge, and the successes are true shining examples of education at its finest. No matter how many obstacles we face, we *are* going in the right direction.

That's what this book — and this chapter especially — is about. The emphasis needs to be shifted from what's supposedly wrong with our educational system to what's right with it, and how to encourage and emulate the people who are doing so much to help the students who need it most. I want to talk about *the Teacher's Teacher* — where these marvelous people came from, what they are like, the obstacles they face, and how they thrive in one of society's most challenging jobs.

From a Special Place

I'm often asked for a concise definition of the Teacher's Teacher. In some ways, that's like asking for a concise explanation of the origin of the universe, but we can narrow it down somewhat. In the simplest terms, the Teacher's Teacher is an individual who loves *people*, and everything else is a subset of or a corollary to that. In particular, of course, the Teacher's Teacher is totally dedicated to his or her students, and never comes into the classroom with predefined notions as to who can learn and who can't. Taking this one step further, the Teacher's Teacher *respects* all people. He or she is committed, comes in early and will stay late, and basically will do whatever it takes to connect with the students who need help the most.

The Teacher's Teacher may look or sound like anyone. He or she may be city bred, rural, suburban, or foreign born, and may come from any ethnic, racial or religious group — but there is a connecting thread. Where they all come from is a belief system. Paul Gounaris, a high school principal, put this in the clearest of terms for me when he said, "Mark, it's *all* about the kids. And it's about believing that *all* people deserve the opportunity to succeed."

I recently met a young man from Cambodia who is a teacher in an administrative graduate program, and he viewed the situation from the perspective of coming from a country that has gone through several governments, most of them oppressive. He was explaining how frustrated he is here trying to raise money and get things done for a special program he has for Cambodian students; but then he added, "As frustrated as I am, here we've got such a great system!" Many Americans seem to lose sight of how fortunate we really are. "I was afraid even to speak in my own home," he recalled, "because we always had that feeling that someone was listening, and people could die just for saying the wrong thing." His expression of support for our system truly hit home. This was quite a different twist for all of us listening, after the hammering of American education and how we're supposedly failing one another.

The measure of a successful teacher is not about test scores. It's about helping the individual experience success, whether that means learning to add, or processing simple fractions or decimals, or discovering a new theory of quantum physics. The Teacher's Teacher is committed to helping all people in their pursuit of self-improvement, regardless of the starting point or the number of revolving doors.

In essence, the Teacher's Teachers are the ones who care. From that simple statement all the rest can be extrapolated. And the fact is that good things are happening. There are a lot of great teachers out there who *are* caring. They don't look at color or gender, and they don't look at ethnic background. They don't look at, or listen to, the naysayers who say that the schools are bad or that nothing can be done. They simply look at *students*. They look at the future. They are the ones who know that every student in their classrooms has a right to succeed, and that education is the primary route to that success.

How many of these truly dedicated teachers are there? And what does the full spectrum of attitudes look like? Of the teachers I've worked with, I can say confidently that most of them are committed and caring. After I conclude an in-service I usually find that about 85% of the faculty will be very positive, upbeat, and getting reinforced from everything we do. About 10% will not have much to say, a response which could be interpreted in many different ways. Then there are about 5%, in any community and in any school, who go out of their way to show that they have no business in the classroom. Those are the ones we hear talking trash, saying that the school stinks and the kids are no good. They reiterate, almost like a mantra, "I'm sick of this," or "I'm burned out."

Sometimes I get openly negative reactions from this last group, as I've described in Chapter 1. We don't need to hold an in-service to identify these teachers, though, because the students are all too ready to point them out. These teachers aren't fooling anyone, no matter how young their students are. I couldn't begin to count how many times I've heard kids say to me, "Mark, you're telling us that no family member, no teacher, no friend, *no one* has the right to put us down. Yet there's a teacher in this school who laughs at us and demeans us. There are a couple of teachers in this building who should hear your lecture."

I do not mean to say that these 5% are bad people, or that they deserve some kind of retribution or humiliation. No one does. But it does seem clear that they are in the wrong place, sometimes doing irreparable harm where they could and should be a force for good. And that's a terrible waste. Anyone can become the Teacher's Teacher, as long as he or she is committed to it. But those who can't, or won't, are in the wrong line of work and should move on, for their own sakes at least as much as for the sake of their students. Finding out that teaching is not where we belong is *not* a failure, or a defeat, and it's certainly not a disgrace. A wise person is honest with him - or herself, and acts accordingly. Therefore, seeking out our true place shows wisdom, courage and maturity, and that is something we can be proud of teaching by example.

I take great pride and optimism from all the dedicated people I've met in the course of my work, all the Teacher's Teachers and those who are well on their way toward that goal. What I'd like to talk about next is how to become the Teacher's Teacher.

Becoming the Teacher's Teacher

As I've said above, many are well on their way to becoming the Teacher's Teacher, and any dedicated and caring teacher can achieve that goal. Many know that they want to achieve it but are not there yet. What can they do to move closer toward their ideal?

In many cases, it's a simple matter of giving voice and action to the principles they already hold dear. Of course it means never allowing themselves to buy into the idea that Johnny or Mary can't learn. But just knowing this is only the beginning. They need to go beyond knowing it to *showing* it, making sure that the students know it as well. Everything a teacher does should reflect that principle — but the simplest and most direct way to communicate this to your students is to tell them. Don't be afraid to say exactly that. "I know that you can learn. I know that you can fulfill your potential. I know that you can achieve great things. I'm here to help, but the greatness lies within you."

By contrast, it's important also to avoid ever buying into the apathy, the insensitivity and the uncaring attitude of the small but very vocal minority who don't belong in teaching. To some extent we become like those we associate with, and repeated exposure can cause their ideas to settle in despite our best intentions. This is a simple fact of human nature. To position ourselves in a successful mode daily, we cannot afford to be in a teachers' room where even one teacher's spewing trash, because it will affect our demeanor and our mindset. It's *poison*, and we've got to stay away from it.

Of course, ongoing education is also a factor in becoming the Teacher's Teacher. Who knows better than the teacher that education is a lifelong process? The Teacher's Teacher is *always* questioning, reevaluating, updating, and finding new material. This is not to suggest that new material is always better than what we have now, but it certainly merits perusing. The teacher who thinks he or she knows all there is to know is definitely not the Teacher's Teacher. The Teacher's Teacher is the one who has that *open* flexibility of self and is always looking for a better way. MaryAnn Matthews, an outstanding teacher in Charlestown, MA, told me, "Mark, I'm always looking for a new angle to connect — for another way to *inspire* them." I know she means it.

Praise, when given in an honest and timely way, is another hallmark of the Teacher's Teacher, and learning to give praise effectively is very important to becoming a better teacher. Teachers need to encourage their students at whatever level they're on, without bias, without ignoring anyone, and without allowing personal feelings to interfere. The great teacher recognizes and delights in a student making the effort, at whatever level. But it's also important to make sure that all your students feel recognized. It's easy to jump to the conclusion that Johnny who just gets things easily and who always gets the "A" may not merit any praise at all. This is just as blind as assuming that "A" students deserve vast amounts of praise regardless of their amount of effort. Mary, who *really* has a tough time getting a passing grade but who made an extraordinary effort and only got a "C," certainly merits some extensive praise and reinforcement — but not in such a way that Johnny feels left out. And what about Joey who simply maintains his "B" average *status quo*? He deserves praise also — and it may inspire him to make a new effort.

Above all, encouragement should be ongoing, and your highest praise has to be *earned*. What's important is to let each student know that we recognize his or her individual accomplishments, whatever they may be. It's wonderful to tell a student that you're aware that he or she worked very hard to study for a test. It's also wonderful to tell a student that you've noticed his or her consistent record of getting good grades, or of maintaining a consistent grade point average. As long as they've accomplished something good or even simply tried to do so, we need to let them know that their efforts did not go unnoticed, and that we're cheering them on.

Is it possible to exceed an appropriate level of praise and do more harm than good? Certainly, but this should never hold us back until we see the warning signs. If you see a student becoming complacent, or ceasing to make an effort, or taking the attitude that she only needs to do what seems to make you happy, then it's time to back off and reassess. More importantly, it's time to communicate to the student exactly what you see happening. When you've done that, you're ready to help empower that student to get back on track and perhaps do even better than before. There's no reason to fear this situation, as long as you are careful to manage it.

One last step to becoming the Teacher's Teacher is through modeling yourself after others: the teachers in your building who seem to connect and who have classrooms where it all works. Those are the classrooms where there's not a lot of disruption, or noise, and where the kids seem to want to be. Those are also the teachers to seek out for company, and for information and advice. What are they doing with their students? What wonderful success stories can they tell? What wonderful feelings can they communicate? What ideals can they illuminate? If they are the Teacher's Teachers, they'll have lots to tell, and will love sharing it.

Is It Ever Just a Job?

There's no questioning the fact that teaching is a job, the same as is delivering the mail or trying a case or fixing a broken pipe. There will be days when even the great teachers have to say "dammit, this is just a job!" just to get some perspective. Is teaching a bigger part of a person's life than some other job would be? And what do we do on the inevitable down days? If we invest so much more of ourselves in our work, don't we risk suffering greater lows along with the higher highs?

First let's look at how we got here. There are people who fall into teaching, just as there are people who fall into any profession, and find that they lucked out and become great at what they're doing. My experience has been that this is an aberration. Most of the great teachers wanted to teach. Although I've worked with some great teachers who told me that they fell into their career and still others who say that teaching chose them — much to their and their students' good fortune — most of the great teachers that I've worked with chose teaching. In any case, the great teachers — the Teacher's Teachers — know that they are where they belong now.

In my opinion, however controversial that may be, great teachers are born. There's a calling from within. I've seen it with young teachers, and with those at the end of their wonderful careers. The Teacher's Teacher simply *has* it. From the beginning they know that they get excited about helping people to learn. And they're constantly looking for that self-improvement which will allow them to help the students improve themselves.

Of course all teachers have their ups and downs. They have their fair share of bad days; and no matter how many funks they help their students out of, that doesn't mean that they can't get into one themselves. Teaching *is* a job, and no job is perfect. Even the greatest level of commitment can't protect us against occasional feelings of frustration. However, there is a cure, and that cure is positive reinforcement. On those inevitable bad days, a great teacher needs to be in association with other positive people who will remind him or her of the bigger picture and the wonderful things that great teachers can do. Just as the negative "vibes" can rub off, so do the positive ones.

If we're sometimes tempted to treat teaching as "just a job" — showing up and doing the minimum rather than giving it our full energy — this may be because it's painful to give so much and see so little reward. We may feel underpaid, and underappreciated by our colleagues, by parents, even by students. What keeps us going when there seems to be little support for what we're trying to do? At times like this, we need to remember how badly our students need us — even the ones who don't show it. Our job may last for decades, but those students have only a few brief years to learn what they need to know, to prepare for everything that life will throw at them.

Even when we aren't getting any positive reinforcement, it's important to remember how important our jobs are. Time after time, I've read letters that show the huge difference a teacher's influence has made, even when the student didn't know it until much later. Many of them are printed in this book.

Ironically, we can also protect ourselves and our love of teaching by not putting unrealistic pressures on ourselves. We may love what we do — it may be the most important thing in our lives — but as I've said before, we need to put failure and obstacles in context. If our job is too all-consuming, then when things go wrong there's nowhere to go to stand back and get perspective. We need to find a balance in our commitment to teaching so that it doesn't take us over and eat us alive.

Finally, on those down days, let's also make it a point to take stock in what we've accomplished. That is the time to dwell on our victories, to take pride in our accomplishments, and to call up a mental picture of every student we know we've helped. At that point, the blahs usually disappear. Today, at this moment, teaching may be just a job, but tomorrow is another day — and another triumph.

When Things Change

A common error made by people in all walks of life is to mistake change for failure. As I say repeatedly throughout this book, we need to give ourselves permission to fail. Winners fail all the time; they just pick themselves up and try again. We cannot keep beating ourselves up about it. However, it's very important to understand that what we are quick to call failure may not be failure at all. It may simply be change.

The students we teach today are not the same as the students we taught a decade ago, or even a few short months ago. They grow as they learn; they mature; they change. Consequently, methods and ideas that worked just recently may not work today, but this is not failure. It is only change. We have changed during this time also, although we may be the last to perceive it. The point is that we must evolve with the changes around us, not be frozen in fear or puzzlement when things don't turn out the way we expected. The dynamics of teaching are part of what makes teaching so rewarding. Watch the changes and try to become more adept at spotting them, both in your environment and in yourself, but don't assume that because things change you have failed. The truth may be exactly the opposite.

This principle applies to other aspects of our lives, and especially to those life changes that may be responsible for many of our down days. We all have lives outside of our profession, and it would be extremely naive to think that we don't bring them into the classroom every morning, just as our students bring theirs. Our finances can take a downturn. Our loved ones may pass away. Relationships may not turn out as we had hoped. Marriage, even the one we were sure would last a lifetime, may end. Are these failures? Not necessarily. Even in those cases (such as finances and marriage) where we do have some control, everything is subject to the inevitable laws of change. We are not the same people that we were when we began these processes many years ago, and what worked for us then may not work for us now.

We must accept the changes in our world and in our lives, with the knowledge that we have done our best — and in the case of the Teacher's Teacher, or anyone who sincerely aspires to be one, that best is very great indeed. Sometimes we will feel pain, or even cause it, but to expect a lifetime or a career free of pain is to avoid the real world. No one can take our triumphs and our successes or all of our good years away from us. Keep them with you in your mind and in your heart, and they will help you get through the changes, with the knowledge that you have helped so many things change for the better. Could you ask for anything more wonderful than that?

Teachers can't feel that they're failures because a student fails, or because changes take matters in an unexpected direction or out of their sphere of influence. If they've tried to the best of their ability, then they should still be proud, because that in itself is a measure of success. In addition, the teacher has to understand that even failure itself can be a *positive* experience, if he or she learns from it and moves on to a higher ground. Only if no learning has taken place has a teacher truly failed. And only if we cover our eyes and ignore the natural course of changes will they ever defeat us.

Conquering the Fear

I started out by talking about fear and how it can hold us back from becoming great teachers. Fear can be disabling if it keeps us from trying new things, aiming higher, taking risks. Overcoming this kind of overwhelming fear is one of the most important steps we can take towards committing to greater excellence.

At the same time, I'm often asked if the fear ever completely goes away, even for the great teachers. My answer is "not really" — and one of the marks of the Teacher's Teacher is his or her ability to accept and live with that fact. There's nothing wrong with fear. We've got to fear the fire because the fire can harm us. It's when we become overwhelmed or crippled by fear that we reduce our potential, along with our emotional and physical well being. The Teacher's Teacher can turn the sources of fear into a force for good — a motive for careful preparation and respect for others, and a source of continuous self-improvement. The good news is that fear need never hold us back from accomplishing our goals. Let's look at some of the most common sources of fear faced by even the greatest of teachers, and at some ways to overcome them.

That First Day of School

It's time. You take a deep breath, square your shoulders, straighten your collar, walk into the first classroom, and there they are. All eyes are focused on you — and you panic. What happens?

This may remind you of the first day that, no longer a student teacher, you walked in to teach your first class. The trouble is that this phenomenon may recur with each new class, year after year. This is not abnormal, and you shouldn't be embarrassed if it happens to you. But you don't have to let it get in your way.

Many things may go through the mind of the veteran teacher as well as the new one. Will I be able to connect? Can I still connect? The dynamic of anxiety is basically the same in both cases, and so are the steps to renewed confidence. First of all, you've got to *want* to connect. Secondly, you've got to believe that you *can* connect. Thirdly, you've got to be open to the fact that what might work with one student, or one class, does not necessarily work with another. The challenges recur — but so do your wisdom and strength in dealing with them. We can step through that *fear* in just the same way as we stepped through the door — with a little honest nervousness, but with the confidence that great things await us on the other side.

Now let's touch on a more delicate issue. Not every educational situation is ideal, and not all students are upstanding citizens. Both men and women teachers may find themselves afraid when looking at an unknown group of young people, many of whom have adult strength and may have violent tendencies. Sadly, sometimes this fear is justified; and if you find yourself in this situation, bolstering your courage and self-confidence is only part of the solution. You must do whatever is necessary, in a non-threatening and non-confrontational manner, to ensure your safety. Take someone with you. Carry a cell phone or a noise alarm. Leave the door open. Make sure that someone outside knows where you are. These are reasonable precautions, and will not communicate an atmosphere of mistrust to your students. After all, self-preservation and personal safety are values that you, as a teacher, wish to inspire in them.

However, always remember the American value of "innocent until proven guilty." Take necessary actions to protect yourself, and then give your students the benefit of your faith. Perhaps that's all that some of them need in order to change their own self-images.

Tragedy in the Classroom

This is many teachers' and many students' nightmare, and we're constantly seeing it on the news. Whether it's an act of violence, a senseless mishap or a destructive act of nature, terrible things do happen within our schools, and they shake our students to the core.

I arrived at Dartmouth High School a couple of days after three young men had forced their way into a classroom and killed a student in front of other students and faculty members. Don King, the principal, was literally in tears when he told me this. He was practically incapacitated by grief, and he felt terribly helpless.

There is no way that any school, anywhere, can totally prevent that type of abomination from taking place. He dealt with it, however, by being honest and open, by sharing his hurt and his sorrow, and by being a guiding force to help the students, faculty and community come together as a group to support one another and the bereaved family. He showed that he was the Teacher's Teacher, and everyone responded in kind. He helped them through it.

One morning when I walked into Coventry High School in Connecticut, I was told that the gentleman who was supposed to be introducing me had committed suicide that morning. I immediately responded that we'd cancel the lecture. The great teachers there, however said, "No, Mark, we'd prefer that you confront the issue and deal with it during the lecture." At that point I rose to the challenge, and we did a salute to the man — not to focus on whatever reasons led him to his untimely demise, but on what a great teacher he *was* and how much he *cared* about the students. It was one of the best sessions I've ever done.

The focus was changed from tragic to positive because of great teachers who chose to confront reality. There are some teachers who refuse to deal with such issues, who will not talk about certain subjects, who because of their own inhibitions and their fear will stay forever inside their comfort zone. It's as if they believe that cutting themselves off from these realities will make reality go away.

Our students will have to deal with reality, every moment of the rest of their lives. Let's empower them to survive their inevitable tragedies by setting a good example.

One-Upmanship: Accepting Our Humanity

One of the most universal, archetypal sources of terror is the fear of embarrassment. It shows up in our dreams in a variety of disturbing (albeit amusing) symbols: being caught in the bathroom, being naked in public, walking in late to a critical meeting we hadn't known about. Of course, for a teacher, one of the most powerful fears is being "shown up" because of something one misconstrued or simply didn't know — usually by a student.

It is true that students love to catch us in mistakes, and it's equally true that some of our students are smarter than we are, or know more about our subject than we do. This is a simple fact that we have to face. Indeed, at some schools, such as Boston Latin and other specialty institutions, it is the rule rather than the exception. It takes a very special Teacher's Teacher to meet that kind of challenge every day!

Lying deep behind that fear is the irrational voice that whispers, "I'm going to be exposed as a charlatan. I am not the great teacher. I am going to be humiliated, discredited and disgraced." That fear has to be confronted along with the realization that we all have our limitations. There are going to be those individuals who appear throughout our lives who are more attractive, stronger, smarter and generally more successful than we are. That fact doesn't lessen our value or our accomplishments in the slightest.

The great teachers are always telling me about a student who solved a technical problem above and beyond their guidance, or who found a meaning in a work of literature or art that had always eluded the teacher. The Teacher's Teachers get a kick out of that. In fact, they see it as a learning experience for themselves and use it in the next class. They never chastise, or betray or belittle, and they certainly don't internalize or take it personally as their failure. The Teacher's Teachers learn from every source, and showing this to their students can convey an invaluable lesson whenever the opportunity arises. They know that their role in the classroom isn't just based on *knowing* more — it's also based on leadership, maturity, and communication. Being able to help even a gifted student learn and grow is the ultimate challenge and joy for the Teacher's Teacher.

A friend of mine teaches grammar, writing and proofreading to adult business professionals (which seems scary enough). She tells me that her students sit poised on the edge of their seats, ready to catch her in the inevitable faulty keystroke or grammatical slip of the tongue; and when they do, they holler it out, point fingers and laugh as hard as they can. "Doesn't that bother you?" I asked her, wondering how well I would handle such intense scrutiny. "No, indeed," she said with a smile. "It shows motivation, interest in the subject, a growing mastery of the principles, and attention to my every word. To a teacher, it's the ultimate compliment!"

We are not gods. We are not perfect or infallible. We are human. Enjoy it.

The Cliffhanger

Of the emotionally challenging moments that a teacher has to deal with, perhaps the most heart-wrenching is commencement and the end of the senior year. We've been caring and supportive. We've done our best. We've brought many of our students farther than they ever thought they could go. And now it's June 15, the students walk out the door and we realize we'll never know what happens to them. How do we simply end the story and say goodbye?

In most cases, it's true that we're never going to know and we can't expect to know; and it's true that it hurts. Teachers confide this to me almost daily. In particular with the seniors whom they will never see again, I see teachers sobbing, in pain, emotionally drained. They did all they could do for their students, and now, for themselves, it's over.

What sustains the great teachers is that they know they made a difference, a contribution to their students' ongoing quest for self-improvement, and that has to be enough. We've made the commitment, and the wonderful results *are there*, even if they're no longer within our sight. Realistically we all know that, and we know that some of our students will move on to true greatness. And the fact is that we *do* see many of the results. Every time we see an advance in science, a beneficial new law, or even a simple act of kindness, we see the hand of the Teacher's Teacher — perhaps not our own, but that of someone very much like us — and we must mentally thank that teacher, just as somewhere another such teacher is thanking us.

The satisfaction has to come in the doing of the job, and in seeing its results in the world around us. And, as strange as it may sound, the satisfaction has to come from the fact that the job is never truly finished, because each year brings in a whole new group of students and the incomparable privilege of being able to begin once again at the beginning. In how many other professions can one truly say that?

Yes, there is sorrow at the separation, but the great teachers don't view their students' leaving them as a loss. They know they've done the best that they could do, and they take their satisfaction from that. Yes, this is a very emotional time, and there's no use pretending that the emotion doesn't exist. But when the Teacher's Teachers see the challenge upcoming — a new class to connect with, ready and waiting — then the picture suddenly looks bright. "Here we go again," they say to themselves with a smile. "We're going to try one more time."

In Summary, but Not in Conclusion

> "A hundred years from now it will not matter the sort of house I lived in, what my bank account was or the kind of car I drove, but the world may be different because I was important in the life of a child."
>
> Anonymous

I want to finish this chapter with a few simple statements that sum up what I see as the essence of the Teacher's Teacher.

The Teacher's Teacher cares.

The Teacher's Teacher shows respect, and self-respect.

The Teacher's Teacher knows that the process of change and improvement is infinite.

The Teacher's Teacher is committed to excellence on a daily basis.

The Teacher's Teacher helps students to think on their own.

And, most of all: the Teacher's Teacher rises to the challenge.

My thanks to all of the Teacher's Teachers who have taught me this. Now it's my turn to say that your kindness, your caring and your commitment were acknowledged and treasured. Please accept this tribute on behalf of all those who have traveled on to other lives but who will always hold students deep in their hearts.

Chapter 4

Who Is a "Special" Student?

As you think back on your years of teaching, some students are probably uppermost in your mind. Perhaps they were especially bright, or had a special talent. Perhaps they had a special need. Perhaps they were those wonderful students who made other people feel special. Or perhaps they made their mark on your life because there was nothing "special" about them at all! Who are the "special" students? All of them!

When I visit Charlestown High School in Boston, I always see Larry Matthews shake hands with his students as they come into the room. In so doing, Larry is showing each and every one of them that he understands that they are individuals deserving of respect. He's showing them that they are special. I couldn't agree more.

As I've stressed many times throughout this book and all across the country in my presentations, every student is unique. Each individual has his or her own "fingerprint" — his or her character, personality, likes and dislikes, nature, soul. But our society has given us labels for "types" of students, and in many cases society's original intentions were good. We need to identify "special needs" so that our schools can get funding for some very important programs. We need to identify "gifted" students so that we can help them qualify for programs that will develop their talents. Still, we have to be very careful about using labels. We need to know when to apply a label, and when to cast it aside. We must allow ourselves and our schools to *group* students only in ways that will benefit them — and to constantly regroup and reshuffle those groups, whenever necessary to keep them beneficial — without ever allowing a *label* to confine or restrict any student.

So — this chapter looks at some of these different *groups* of students, and the ways in which you can be most helpful in guiding them toward reaching their full potential.

"Special Needs"

When I met with Russ Norton, the principal of Sandwich High School, after my presentation there this past February, I had a unique experience to ask him about. There had been two young men in the front row of the auditorium who were especially expressive and responsive when I told the group, "No one has the right to put you down. No teacher, no family member, no friend." One of these fellows in a football jersey actually stood up and cheered, 'That's right! Right on!' I didn't know what to make of it. Well, Russ fell apart laughing. He said, "Mark, do you know who those two fellows are? Both of them are 22 years old, and they're learning disabled. We have a special program here at Sandwich High."

I was astounded. In a lot of schools, students over age 21 aren't even allowed in the building; but in this case, great teachers and caring people have surrounded them and continually reinforced the strengths these young men had. Now they were graduating as part of the senior class. Russ Norton continued, "They are going to be extremely productive citizens, living fulfilling lives." What more can anyone ask?

These are so-called "learning disabled" people. They were fabulous. They were respectful, they were responsive, they were articulate and they were enthusiastic. It was a privilege to have met them.

My personal feeling is that there's no such thing as learning "disabled." One group of students may learn *differently*, but we all do that. No two of us are alike. To give a student a label

suggesting that he or she cannot learn is to place an unfair
burden on the student, the teacher and the school. My
experience is that in the schools where these students are treated
like the worthy individuals that they are — not like losers or
problems in the school system, or like there is something wrong
with them — they blossom, and they have tremendous potential
for success. These two young men are a case in point because
they are adults who chose to be there and who exceeded the only
expectations that mattered: their own.

Unfortunately, many groups of students encounter obstacles
created by labels. I'll mention some of these labels only once and
then discard them as the irrelevancies that they are: physically
handicapped, developmentally disordered, chronically ill,
disfigured or otherwise malformed. *Unlike.* The difficulties that
these groups of students face — or, rather, that some systems
place upon them — stem from a familiar source: the discomfort
some people have with those different from themselves. We
have learned, slowly and painfully, that differences such as race,
religion, ethnicity, etc., have no place in our assessment of
another human being. However, many of us still have yet to
achieve this realization when it comes to those we view as less
fortunate in their physical attributes, and we experience
discomfort around them. We shy away from meeting their eyes.
We fidget. We move too far away to let them pass. In other
words, we still give in to negative emotions, such as pity, or
helplessness, or *fear* of the very notion of being less fortunate.
Should we be surprised to learn that these students do not see
themselves that way?

I see these students in high schools all across the country. In
particular, I recall a young man in a wheelchair who had the
mobility of only one hand, and whose total body size was maybe
two and a half feet. He came down to the front of the
auditorium, made eye contact with me and then spoke up when
I asked who is responsible in our lives for what we do. He said,
"I'm responsible for myself, and there are no limits." Looking
me square in the face, he continued, "There are no limits to what

I can achieve. I believe I can do it." Some would have seen his situation as very limiting, but he didn't see that. He didn't view himself as being paralyzed or crippled or deformed. Later he told me that he was going to college; that he had a loving family; that the kids in the school were great. This young man wasn't focused on what he couldn't do but on what he could and would do. He had a warm and wonderful smile, and he gave the impression of a very attractive and confident person who would go far. Special needs? He didn't think so, and I'm willing to bet that time proved him right.

Are there students with special needs? Certainly — but often these are needs that our school systems created. For so-called budgetary reasons, too often very disparate groups of students are lumped together into voc-ed programs called "special." These programs may group such diverse individuals as physically impaired, learning or developmentally different, and behavioral problem students into one classroom and attempt to teach them the same thing, at the same time and in the same way. This benefits no one. Students, teachers, aides and planners are all working at cross purposes, and the result is a total fiasco. No one learns, and in many cases serious harm can be done. Compounding the problem, these groups are often assigned to the least experienced and seasoned teachers who find themselves helpless despite their good intentions.

This phenomenon has been given the horrible name "dumping ground syndrome." I'd like to think that no school actually has such an attitude; but the simple truth is that *good schools don't do this*. A good school is one in which the *individual* is respected, and every student is put into the learning environment that is best for him or her. Good educators understand that putting such a diverse group together under the guise of budget management is unthinkable. It doesn't work, and it's up to all of us to work to change such a system wherever we see it. That's a major part of being the Teacher's Teacher.

For the vast group of students called "special needs," the Teacher's Teacher is someone who has learned a lot from his or her students, and vice versa. That wonderful young man who told the assembly that "there are no limits" certainly had known the Teacher's Teacher, and they both had benefited tremendously, as did those who followed. All of these students need you, and you need them.

How can you help these students to be their best? By meeting their eyes, and shaking their hands. By showing you understand and believe in what they can accomplish. And by letting them know that their specialness comes from within, and that their uniqueness — like everyone else's — is something to be treasured.

"Special Gifts"

Glen Esterbrook, head of science at Boston Latin, America's oldest high school, said to me, "Mark, you go into some tough schools, in some very tough neighborhoods. But have you ever considered how tough it is to be at Boston Latin, where we're sometimes trying to teach students who know more about the subject matter than we do?" As we've already seen, one of the greatest challenges involved in teaching gifted students is accepting the fact that we, as teachers, are going to be constantly and increasingly challenged — and by all our students!

Most schools have programs for students who excel academically or in some specific area, but the job of the Teacher's Teacher for these students only *begins* there. If I could sum up this section in two words, those words would be "don't assume." Erroneous assumptions are the greatest handicap for gifted students and for those who teach them. Here are some of the most common misconceptions of which we all need to beware:

   ...that gifted students "have it made"
   ...that these students don't need our help
   ...that social class or family money plays a part in giftedness
   ...that one type of gift is superior to another

Our society, for better or for worse, places a greater emphasis on some types of skills than on others. The attorney is rewarded more than the carpenter. The athlete is valued above the artist. Surgical skills are considered more important than auto repair skills — but what of the surgeon on his way to the hospital who suddenly finds that his car has broken down? All of these skills are needed for our society to function and flourish.

It's up to us to foster and encourage giftedness in our students in whatever form it may take. Society's standards change frequently, after all, and the picture may look very different only a few short years from now. One of my favorite examples of this was told to me by Joe Golec, a former football coach at a Massachusetts high school. A young man he considered to be an extraordinary player was awarded a full college scholarship, but to the coach's amazement he turned it down. This young man loved cars and engines, and just wanted to work with automobiles. Being the true professional that he is, the coach helped the young man into a voc-tech training program in auto mechanics, but nonetheless felt disappointed that the young man wasn't going to "college." "I met the young man again five years later while I was renting a beach cottage," Joe recently wrote to me. "I asked which cottage he was renting, and he replied, 'I *own* those four along the beach.' Well, he had managed to become the head supervisor for a major communications company's entire fleet of trucks. He likes his job. I'm still renting." Who is to say that outstanding ability in one field is not as praiseworthy as excellence in another? Certainly not the Teacher's Teacher!

What of the high correlation between affluent areas and gifted student programs? We'd be fooling ourselves if we said that as many gifted students are identified in inner-city schools as in the suburban and the private schools. But it's not that they aren't there; it's that often the school systems don't look, or are not encouraged to do so. We need to look, and look hard, in order to do our best by these students. By the same token, we can't give in to reverse bias and assume that the wealthy private school student in the advanced placement program doesn't deserve to be there. That may be just as invalid and destructive an assumption. Of course, many times attitudes do play a part. We've probably all heard about the gifted inner-city student who drops out of school or simply gives up because she feels the deck is stacked against her — that "nobody from here has ever made it, so why should I try?" By contrast, there are the students from wealthy families who simply assume that their futures are all set and that they deserve it — those lucky enough to be born on third base but think they hit the triple. Both cases are equally tragic. The former may refuse to walk through the door to success unless we can manage to help her open it; and the latter may find himself stranded and helpless with no marketable skills if the family business suddenly fails. These students definitely need our help, and in more than academics. Good teachers, above all, teach *values*.

Finally, we need to understand that "gifted" is a label; and like any other label, it can help or hurt. Gifted students can be very lonely; and they can be seriously burdened by other people's expectations that they never asked for. They may suffer because of the misconception that a talent in one area means that they should be equally good in others. Students can burn themselves out trying to meet expectations like these. Comparisons are just as dangerous for the students on the favorable end of the comparison. Gifted students can also suffer greatly trying to meet unrealistic or excessive demands of parents, or their own impossibly high standards. They can become convinced that once they achieve a certain level they can never let themselves drop below it. That's absurd — we all have our highs and lows. Be aware of this syndrome; breakdowns and even suicides can result.

Be careful not to isolate the gifted student. Let him or her experience life. These young people have much to learn from their fellow students as well. Gifted students are special, just as all students are special, but this does not make them better, and they need to understand this. Also, remember to go out of your way to find giftedness in areas where many educators don't think to look for it: manual/trade skills; empathy; understanding; the ability to bring out the best in others. These are gifts also. Are these young people the future Teacher's Teachers?

Look for the truly gifted student in any way that a gift may manifest itself. Look everywhere. Look constantly. Help them to find their unique greatness.

"Special Situations"

Students bring a vast number of circumstances into the classroom with them: their home life; their histories; their concern with relationships, gangs, abuse, violence, addictions and more. Special situations are a fact of their lives and ours.

A student recently wrote on a comment card about my presentation, "This is going to help me with my drug problem." This student deserves tremendous credit for mentioning his drug problem as a simple statement of fact. Not "a possible drug problem." Not "my [unspecified] problem." Not "students who have drug problems." In saying "my drug problem," he has taken ownership and therefore responsibility. I'm willing to bet that he will succeed in conquering his addiction, with help and treatment.

Whether our students' problems are drugs, or alcohol, or food, or sex, dealing with them directly and honestly is the key, both for them and for us. The more that people hide from it, or pretend it doesn't exist, the more destructive it can become. Deal with it directly. Let the student feel safe in telling us, "I have a problem. I'm anorexic. I'm bulimic. I abuse heroin. I'm an alcoholic. I eat constantly. I look for sweets all the time. Help me." When people feel comfortable in their surroundings and know that they will be accepted, they're much better able to start conquering the enemy. We can't solve society's addictions, but we can make a very good beginning, one student at a time.

As teachers, we already have a head start because our students are *in school*. Sometimes I see students nodding out on me and I'm told by other students, "Hey, Mr. Mainella, I apologize for my buddy, but you know, he's a junkie and he falls asleep." My response to that is, "God bless him — at least he's in school, not out on a street corner shooting up." We're here for these students, and we have a chance to help. Who's there for the ones on the outside?

What many students see every day is a nightmare: stabbings, shootings, prostitution and death. But when I go into even the toughest schools in America, what I see are *good kids*. These are truly some of my best kids, the most appreciative, the most respectful and responsive. On the average, I get far more "please" and "thank you" responses in so-called "tough" schools than in many of the private schools and affluent communities. Take that for what it's worth.

The horror is that the people who are really caught up in that nightmare world don't go to school, at least not on the high school level. The ones who are in school are there because they want to beat the odds, and they know that education is their only way out. We need to do everything we can to support that, and to constantly show them that they've made the right decision. That support can make a world of difference.

After one lecture a young lady came up to thank me, and the principal immediately rushed over to ask, "What did she say?" I explained that she had simply said thank you, and that she really felt good coming here. He sighed and nodded. "She wasn't going to come," he said, "but I asked her to, knowing what you do." Her mother had killed her live-in lover the night before. But the student showed up at school an hour early, knowing the principal was going to be there — knowing that there was someone who was going to be empathetic, sympathetic, understanding. This was truly a great school. Why? There's no big mystery to that. "We love the kids," the principal continued. "She comes out of an environment where there is no safety, where there is no sense of warmth, of comfort, of listening, of caring. She knows that this is a safe place for her to be."

We think — or like to think — that everyone grows up the same way. "Good morning, dear. How are you doing? What do you want for breakfast? Have a good day. Have you got your homework done?" The reality is that a good portion of kids get up in the morning and they're cold and hungry. There's no one there, or if they're greeted at all it's with an obscenity and a boot in the rear end, and told to "get out of my face." *This happens in every school, not just in the inner city.* We can't undo the damage done, but we can provide a safe area, a comfort zone, and some understanding. We can let them know that healing *is* possible, and we can help them find the professionals who will help them to begin. And, if we all do this, we can also help to break the chain so that these students' children will have a much better life.

"Simply Special"

Traditionally, a lot of our attention goes to the students at both ends of the spectrum: the high scorers and the lowest, the most gifted and the most academically challenged and the most athletic and the most severely handicapped. Certainly these students deserve our attention, but what's wrong with this picture? We may have forgotten about the ones in the middle.

These are the students who don't have great sports prowess. They don't get the accolades. They don't perform terribly well academically, but they don't do very poorly either. They're not extremely attractive or unattractive, and they're not the stars of the school play or the glee club soloists. They're not troublemakers, and they're never kept for detention. They don't run for class officer or try out for the cheerleading team. You never need to send a note to their parents. In short, they quite often get lost in the shuffle. I call these hundreds of thousands of students the "simply special." And they are.

It's easy to connect with a bright, motivated student; and it can be easy to connect with a so-called problem student, because oftentimes they will reach out. But the student who needs you the most may be neither of these. How do you find and connect with these students? The answer may surprise you.

The great teachers have taught me that there is a way, and that it can be very easy! Just *looking at your students* can be an important first step. There are some teachers who never make eye contact with their students in the classroom. By virtue of looking past the students — over their heads, at a wall, or simply into thin air — they have effectively stated to those students that they do not exist in that classroom. But all of those students are there, with their individual personalities, their interests and disinterests, their likes and dislikes, and, above all, their need to be acknowledged. Each one is a person deserving of attention and respect. Making a connection with each and every one of them can be as simple as *making eye contact* — with a little smile or a nod, just to tell the individual students that they're part of the play. You're showing them that they're in the class, and that you see and respect them, as a truly great teacher does.

In sum, all we have is each other; and we only have the present moment to show that we know that. If we stay focused on this wonderful principle, then as the young man in the assembly pointed out, there are no limits to what we can achieve.

Are we kind? Are we courteous? Are we sensitive? Are we listening? If so, then we can be confident for our students and for what their future holds.

Chapter 5

Looking for What Doesn't Exist

It would be nice if every student were responsive, and if every teacher were dedicated ... if every school had all the funding it needs ... and if our lives weren't subject to outside forces that shove us off the track despite our good intentions. It would be nice if what we did always worked, and if people easily recognized what works and what doesn't. A lot of this would be really nice. But the simple fact is — if we keep looking for what does not exist, we're going to be disappointed.

In fact, although high standards and hopes are very important, when they're unrealistically high they can ironically foster an attitude of cynicism — the negative attitude of the disappointed idealist. For people like this, nothing is ever good enough. But isn't this just a convenient excuse for not trying? These nonexistent things become like decoys, turning our heads away from what we can really achieve with what's really there.

In this chapter I'm going to focus on some of these decoys and how they keep us trapped in negative attitudes — and how we can learn to look beyond them.

The Student Who Doesn't Exist

The Student Who Doesn't Exist is walking down the halls of our schools every day. At least one would think so, since many entire school systems seem to be designed for him ... or her. That's the student who is of average height, attractive, motivated, economically secure and always very, very interested. He or she has an American-sounding name (whatever that is), and grew up in an English-speaking household. He or she scores well on standardized tests, participates in the expected after-school activities and goes home to a loving two-parent household. This student is "your typical student". Right? *No* — in fact, this picture couldn't be more wrong.

In many of the high schools that I visit, there are multiple languages spoken. In an inner-city school, it's not atypical to hear a dozen different languages or more. Therefore, the challenge of the decade and those to come is in dealing effectively with this diversity, and with people who come from cultures that are entirely different from what we're used to. Teachers have said to me in recent years, "it's just not what it used to be" — but I wonder if they know how interesting a statement that is. Their "what used to be" was a certain socio-economic group, the so-called middle-American white upper-class student, usually male, that the academic arena catered to. Academicians were trained to help *these* students maximize their potential, and many of them never questioned that training. The academicians themselves were most likely Caucasian Americans who also came from middle - or upper-class backgrounds, and whose families were well educated and encouraged them to pursue higher education.

How accurate really was this picture? Not very accurate, even in the middle years of this century, despite what we saw on "American family" TV. After all, America has always been a land of diversity — the difference is that it has recently become socially acceptable to acknowledge it. What has changed? Not the student, but what the teacher expects to see when he or she walks into class every morning. Today, we recognize that the majority is not the stereotypical white middle-class American, but the culturally, racially, linguistically diverse student who is in need of the same support, reinforcement and encouragement as your typical student of the 1950s. What hasn't changed? That phantom student — the Student Who Doesn't Exist, but around whom much of our educational system is still structured.

Educators who are looking for this student are going to find that their efforts are largely ineffective, because the object of those efforts does not exist.

Similarly, teachers may be looking for what does not exist if they expect a student to come into their class brimming over with enthusiasm. An English teacher chose to be an English teacher; an English student did not choose to be in an English class. Teachers must understand this and be prepared to convey the value of their subject. This may extend to conveying the value of education itself, especially if no one has helped the student to see this before.

What about failure? This is just a natural part of being human. Students *and teachers* have to understand that they must sometimes allow themselves to fail; and teachers must also be willing to allow their students to fail occasionally. Winners fail all the time — but they pick themselves up. This is true greatness of character.

The best students succeed with or in spite of all our efforts. The students who are least receptive, who come from the most negative situations, and who don't fit the pre-measured mold left over from the 1950s TV sit-coms — *these are the ones who need our commitment the most.*

The Environment That Doesn't Exist

Are you looking for fairness, equality, an atmosphere without prejudice? How about justice, or decisions based on merit rather than expediency? Again, you're going to be disappointed. These factors are not within our control; and bigotry, barriers and restrictions are everywhere. What we must do to is take control of our own destiny, avoid falling prey to the negative, and try as sincerely as we can to remove ourselves from being part of that play.

Part of this environment is our comfort zone. This is the place we've set up to protect ourselves, where we hide and where we

feel safe. We perceive it because we want to, but it isn't really
there. Hiding from the challenges won't make them go away —
we've got to understand that and get beyond it.

I recently presented a career-change opportunity to a friend of
mine. The opportunity involved a job which did not offer
traditional security. It was a risky proposition, but there was
great potential for success. His response to me was, "Look at
your own situation. You have no security. You work from year
to year, not knowing if you're going to have a deal next year. I
can't work that way. I want — I *need* — security." Therein lies
the point. That is how we limit our potential: looking for what
doesn't exist, wanting to have that constant comfort zone. There
is no such thing.

People who are willing to operate outside of their comfort
zone have far greater opportunities than those looking for
security, or those looking for someone to take care of them. We
have to take care of ourselves. We must get up in the morning,
commit to excellence and do the best that we can on any given
day. So, if your goal is to never leave this comfort zone,
understand the limits that you're putting on your future.
However, if your goal is to ultimately be the best you can be,
you must be willing to operate outside of your comfort zone
with the reality of failure being present at any given time.
Winners fail on occasion; they learn from their mistakes and
move on. Give yourself permission to fail. Fear of failure inhibits
your potential. Winners are constantly re-accessing their
situation. They gather more information that allows them to
make another choice on their redirection and find a way to
succeed. What is important in establishing a fulfilling and truly
successful career is a love for one's work. We can't give to others
what we don't possess. Love your job ... or find another one.

Excuses That Don't Exist

Some people keep looking for solutions everywhere but in themselves. Many of those people will keep on looking ... forever.

We're constantly being told about the problems in our society: alcohol abuse, crime, the divorce rate, and that our schools are not producing functionally literate, productive people. But these are symptoms. One of the major problems underlying these symptoms is that most people do not like what they're doing for a living — and that makes them unhappy with their lives.

Recent occupational surveys tell us that as many as three out of four workers hate their jobs, and wish they were doing something else. How did this come about? Most people have allowed themselves to be *led* through their lives and their decisions, by parents, family members, spouses, friends ... *and* teachers. In most cases, all meant well. The reality, though, is that very few people give much thought — in fact, spend any time at all — focusing on their true strengths, interests, and on what they're really good at.

There is greatness in every human being. But unfortunately, most people never take the time to figure out what their true greatness is. They allow themselves to fall into a career that they believe will give them financial security and the ability to buy things to make themselves feel good: a home, a car, clothes, jewelry, toys, all the material goods that we're told we must have to be successful. Certainly, there's nothing wrong with any of these things, but they don't give us what we really need. *We need to feel good about what we're doing on a daily basis.* We need to know that we're making a contribution, that people are listening to us, that people care about us. If we can't do that, we fail, and we're looking for reasons that don't exist.

This isn't anything new. Socrates said, almost three hundred years before the birth of Christ, "The answer to our life's concerns are internal. Know thyself." Most people, when asked, "How's it going?" respond by saying, "Hey, I'm getting by."

Sadly, what this really means is that they never gave themselves the opportunity to know what they could have been. The good news is that it's never too late. They can start now.

And what about those people who have been allowed to lead us where we don't want to go? Why have we set up our lives to meet their goals? One of my colleagues, Rita Davenport, says, "If you knew how little time people spent thinking about you, you wouldn't waste any of your precious time worrying about what they're thinking." The only persons we have to measure ourselves against are ourselves.

Attitude, Attitude, Attitude

Many people are caught in an endless negative cycle. They get up every day focused on the down-side of life. Think of this as a negative "mirror syndrome": how we see ourselves in the mirror each morning is basically how other people see us throughout the day. When people look in the mirror and see an image they don't respect — when they don't care about themselves, when they're not pursuing self-improvement — that's exactly what other people will see. And when those "mirror syndrome" captives are teachers, the consequences can be far-reaching indeed. What will their students see? What will the young people learn to see in themselves?

No one is willing to invest in that type of person — the "I can't do it's" of the world. We've all heard the expression "excuses are for losers." What that really means is that losers need excuses to justify why they think they can't change — for example, "my ethnic background", "my racial background", "my gender", "I come from a dysfunctional family", "I'm not college material." This is a form of self-sabotage, in which they find a way to blame others and thereby preserve the *status quo*. It's true that nothing is likely to change in a situation like that.

The key to maintaining a positive attitude, which is what it takes to overcome this negativism, is constantly reaffirming within one's self, "I can do it. I can do it. I'm every bit as good as anyone else. I can. And I will." This does take practice, and it needs to be worked at. We can't exercise just once in a while and expect physical well-being; and the same concept applies to our positive sense of self. We can't just say the words occasionally. When we get up in the morning and look in the mirror, we've got to respect ourselves. We've got to care about ourselves. We've got to be willing to constantly seek self-improvement. Then others will see us in a positive light.

Why isn't this as easy as it sounds? In many cases it's because we're being strongly influenced, for better or for worse, by the people around us. We need those people to be enthusiastic and committed to self-improvement, both theirs and ours. Unfortunately, the people who are most likely to put us down are often the ones that we're closest to. It's a difficult proposition, but it's absolutely imperative that we look those individuals in the eye and state our feelings. "Please don't speak to me that way. It's demeaning." "That makes me feel bad." "I accept positive, constructive criticism, but I will not accept a put-down." "I will not allow myself to be deprecated. If you can't say something positive to me, something constructive in terms of my self-improvement, then I do not want to be in your presence."

We cannot afford to be around anyone who is so insecure, who feels so bad about themselves that they must constantly find ways to put other people down, whether through busting or simple self-aggrandizement. Stay away from the "buster."

Everyone can benefit from the message of this chapter, but it has an especially profound importance for us as teachers. As I've reiterated many times, the basic thrust of this book is about finding something that you truly love doing; most people never do. They spend their lives escaping reality because their reality isn't what they want it to be.

But you've already overcome that tremendous hurdle. You've succeeded where most of the world fails. The teachers who love teaching, who respect and care about their students, elicit from them a most positive response. Those students who are taught with respect will return that respect a thousand fold. I've seen this many, many times. And unfortunately, I've also seen the other side of that coin. In my presentations, when a student gets up and uses an obscene gesture or throws a chair across the auditorium, I look beneath the surface to find out what may have caused it. Almost invariably I find that the individual who was responsible for bringing me in was less than committed, less than caring; or that, in fact, the individual who brought me in did care, but a negativism permeates the air, the atmosphere in the school is oppressive, and people are being told what they can't do, not what they can, or the student is living in a very negative, uncaring or even violent household.

On the other hand, when I see a group of students who carry themselves with respect, and who show and even glow with respect — which is most of the time — I'm reminded of everything that's right about our school system, and that the Teacher's Teachers can be everywhere. What more wonderful and valuable attitude could you ever hope to teach? Respect, self-respect, honor, caring and excellence do exist. Never give up looking for them.

Chapter 6

Getting the Most from All Students

We've already discussed "categories" of students. Now let's get beyond them and continue to focus on the *students*, not the labels that have been assigned to them. Most importantly, how do we ensure each student's development to his or her fullest potential? There's no easy answer — in fact, even attempting to do so is difficult, time consuming and often very frustrating. But the Teacher's Teacher is willing to do whatever it takes to bring out the best in each and every one of them. And that very important Teacher's Teacher in a particular student's life is — or can be — you.

Making the Connection

First, always recognize that each student is unique. Now is the time to disregard any and all labels put on your students, regardless of the source or the original intent. Forget the fact that you've been assigned to teach the Special Needs Kids or the Gifted Students or the Troublemakers or the Good Kids. Once you're inside the classroom and the bell rings, you're on. You need to be ready to meet each student on his or her own terms, regardless of how you may perceive those circumstances.

You must try as hard as you can to connect individually with each student. It's unreasonable to assume that you'll know the intimate details of each student's life; as teachers, you have only

a few moments out of each day to get to know your class.
Therefore it is so important to stay focused on the moment!
Make the most of any chance you have to be kind and courteous.
I know these words may be overused, but when I practice them I
feel successful in my life. When I don't, I feel bad. Remember the
Golden Rule? You'd be surprised at how many people don't
know what that is. We must do unto others as we would have
them do unto us — professionally, personally, and in every
aspect of our lives.

But more than this, on both the personal and practical levels,
teachers need to be givers. Givers read the eyes and see inside
the character. They tell us what we desperately need to hear.
They care about other human beings. As givers, teachers need to
inspire, to ignite that latent individually-motivated spark inside
each student. The only way to do this successfully is to
understand and accept all the circumstances each child brings to
the classroom, no matter how difficult they may seem. When
people feel comfortable in their surroundings and know that
they will be accepted, not rejected or ostracized, they are far
more open and ready to succeed.

Because of this, teachers have incredible power in the
classroom. Especially for many young students, the teacher may
seem like a surrogate parent. The teacher seems to have all the
answers and can take on a godlike role in a child's mind. A word
from the teacher can bring complete affirmation, or devastating
criticism. As the Teacher's Teacher, you can use this power for
the students' benefit, to make connections with them. Make
some sort of personal contact. That could be as simple a gesture
as a nod, or a little smile. Make eye contact. Listen to what each
student is saying; really listen. Show each one you care through
your enthusiasm. The connection you make with your students
is what keeps them focused, keeps them wanting to learn,
wanting to make you proud of them.

How far should a teacher go to establish such a connection
with a child? Getting the balance between making contact and
being intrusive takes tact and sensitivity. You can communicate

warmth and caring without overreaching into an inappropriate intimacy. A personal touch — something as basic as a handshake — can be a powerful way of communicating concern and interest. As I stated in Chapter 4, Larry Matthews at Charlestown High School shook hands with his students. This is his way of acknowledging each student. The smallest of actions can reassure a student that he or she is an important part of the play. You don't have to be friends with a student to impart the importance of the subject matter or make them feel important. And while connecting may mean being theatrical to hold their attention in the classroom, it doesn't have to mean going to extremes — we don't need to take an attitude of "I would do anything to connect." But things like spending extra time with a student after hours, working on a student's weak subjects, or helping a student come to terms with a difficult family situation, can make all the difference. Just remember that even the best intentions can be misconstrued — our society is often governed by suspicion, and often without cause. Meet in public places such as a library or cafeteria, and never make a student feel that you're taking advantage of his or her trust.

Some studies of student attitudes have shown that up until the fourth or fifth grade, children have a tremendous sense of self. They believe "I can do anything" — be a superman, climb a mountain, be a doctor, nurse or candlestick maker. But these same studies tell us that by the junior high school years these attitudes have completely reversed. "I can't do it. I'm not college material. I'm not good enough." Each of our interactions with children is a new chance to prove to them that they are important, and capable, and worthy of attention and respect. Teachers can use their power to build character or to break it; but the Teacher's Teacher will always find the means to nurture these young spirits. Teachers have the daunting task of guiding a child's development, both personally — building character, honesty, integrity and respect — and practically, by helping a child identify his strengths and explore the ways in which he will become a productive member of society.

Tim Evers, a guidance counselor at East Lyme High School in Connecticut, is one of the Teacher's Teachers who are very good at this. He would never pressure a student to go into a particular field. Instead he presents options in line with the student's own interests and talents; thus, the student going off to cosmetology school gets as much attention as the one going to Harvard. That student comes to know that these limitations are those that are self-imposed. Based on there own realistic self-assessment, if a student says they can do it, the odds are that they will.

Being a Good Leader: Show Respect, Get Respect

Another aspect of getting the most from your students is cultivating their respect — and this means showing them respect yourself. By demonstrating the give and take of *mutual* respect, you're helping them learn one of the essentials of life.

One fundamental piece of leadership groundwork for the Teacher's Teacher is to set an example as a good role model. Knowing that we are and will always be role models for our students, how do we present ourselves? We convey our sense of self to others by our choices of self-expression — the things we do and say. Like it or not, the first impression we make on another individual is usually a visual one; they see us before they hear us speak. For instance, I believe a teacher has an obligation to be dressed appropriately. Many teachers don't take the time to assess their own appearance, or its effect on others. Still others don't respect the students enough to put on a suit, or a shirt and tie, and then quite often they are the ones who are most taken aback by the students' appearance. If you dress professionally — and granted, "appropriate" dress has different meanings according to where you teach — you send a strong message to students about the importance of self-respect. The students will know that these teachers like themselves and their chosen profession, that they want to be there, and that they respect the students in their class.

Another important aspect of leadership is reinforcement: conveying praise and criticism. We've already seen how important positive reinforcement is, but it's worth emphasizing again. We know that we get the most out of people through positive reinforcement. So why do so many teachers focus on the bad behavior instead of the good? Perhaps because the things we don't like are always more obvious and more irritating. We feel compelled to respond. But the Teacher's Teacher will actively seek out good behavior and reinforce it, whether it's a homework assignment completed on time, a passing grade or just showing up for class every day for a week. Never overlook the obvious or take a student's good behavior for granted! *Don't assume that because something is "the norm" then we don't have to recognize or acknowledge it.* Recognize what is an accomplishment for each of your students, and applaud their efforts to improve — or even their efforts to simply maintain the *status quo*.

Conversely, when you do need to reprimand or correct a student, the way you do it can make a huge difference. In some high schools, I still see teachers scolding humiliated students in classrooms full of their peers. That is not the place to take corrective measures. Remember that you are in the business of building character, not dismantling it, and humiliating a student can leave deep wounds. It can also damage your rapport with the student, sacrificing the trust and respect that you work so hard to build. When you take the time to talk privately to a student, you show them that you respect them and care enough to work with them. You're treating them like an adult, not like a naughty child.

The private sector works the same way. I often work with managers to help them get the most out of their employees. When an employee does something wrong, the good manager takes him or her aside, explains the inappropriateness of the behavior, issues a reprimand and discusses a plan for improvement — all behind closed doors.

Always the Sunny Side Up?

When I talk to teachers about getting the most from their
students, I use the Long-Lasting Battery Syndrome as an
analogy. Everyone has bad days; but when your battery drains
down, it won't help to call in a friend with another drained
battery. Stay away from those who *always* bring you down.
Instead, seek out that never-say-die battery that has all the
power, and lets you recharge from it. When you feel down on
yourself or your job, don't berate yourself — it happens to all of
us at some point. The key to getting past it is to surround
yourself with people who are upbeat, positive thinkers. Re-
energize yourself on their juice. Positive people focus on what
they can do, not what they can't do, even temporarily. Position
yourself where there are positive, loving, caring, giving, sharing
human beings — people with smiles on their faces.

Whenever problems start to get the best of you, put them on
the back burner and get focused on your students. I have heard
administrators say out loud, "I hate these kids, and this school is
terrible. We aren't educating students, we're containing them."
But for every one of those, I can name dozens of others who are
on fire about their schools. Dr. Anderson at Seekonk High School
in Massachusetts is such a person. He has told me every year for
21 consecutive years that his school's students are the best of all.
He'll tell me freely how he loves the school and he works with
the best people. These are the people who fire up the students
and they are the ones to seek out when you're feeling drained.

Finally, one of the best ways to get the most out of your
students is to invest heavily in yourself. Great teachers devote
tremendous amounts of time and effort to refining their skills
and their own innate abilities. They use precious summers,
weekends and holidays to take courses, participate in workshops
and attend training sessions, all for the increased good that
they'll bring to their students. The great teachers are willing to
extract themselves from the "comfort zone" that sets in after a
few years on the job. Some teachers take the tack that they know

their material; they teach the same thing every year, so what's new to learn? Just like your students, you can always learn something new, and truly great teachers find their power zone by stretching themselves. Yes, that may be uncomfortable at first, especially because of the insecurity that comes with exploring new territory. But when you drag yourself out of the comfort zone then you rise to the challenge, and your students learn from your actions, not just your words.

Sylvester Stallone, in the first *Rocky* movie, used boxing as a metaphor to capture the essence of this point, to move himself out of his comfort zone. He used the line again and again, "take your best shot," suggesting that every individual has the opportunity to take responsibility for his or her own life, to improve on present circumstances. Most people never give themselves the chance to take their best shot; they live in the fear that they might fail. So as a teacher, it all comes back to being a good role model. To ask your students to work hard to achieve the best they can achieve, show them that you are willing to fight the same battle yourself.

Stand up and be counted. Your students will follow.

Self-Esteem Builders

Here are some things you can do, every day that will make a big difference to your students' self-esteem:

Smile when you see them.

Greet them by name.

Listen to them when they talk.

Let them know you missed them when they're absent.

Recognize their special talents, even those that don't show up on a report card.

Give each one a chance to succeed in at least one small way every day.

Praise them when they do something right.

If you don't like something they do, help them understand that you still like and respect them.

Show them that they have a lot of options for the future, and that they can set their own goals.

Encourage them to aim high.

Try to reach each student with at least one of these self-esteem builders every day. They build stronger people and stronger communities.

Chapter 7

The Measure of Success

At the very beginning, I said this book was about success —
about losing our fear and committing ourselves to excellence,
and teaching our students how to do the same. Now that we've
looked more closely at the ins and outs of teaching, it's time to
take another look at the idea of success, how we can measure it,
and how it applies to our students and ourselves.

When asked, almost anyone will tell you that the measure of
success today is largely money. Our society is very materialistic
right now, and the people who make the most money are
presented as role models in the media, regardless of the morality
of their actions.

I want to make two important points here. First, it wasn't
always that way — and since our development as a society tends
to be cyclical, before too long that *status quo* will change. Second,
and similarly, it used to be that scholarship and goodness were
valued items, while today they're almost ignored. Is that
discouraging to both teachers and students? Should it be?

If a person makes a lot of money, then *chances are* that person
is successful. On the other hand, many very successful
individuals will never join the ranks of the rich, and many of
those are today's teachers and some of their best students.
Certainly I'll be among the first to jump up and shout that
teachers should be paid much more than they are — but the
point is that real success is not a matter of money, or status, or
things. What is the true measure of success? Let's look at some of
the amazing wealth of possibilities.

Our Notions of Success

> "The quality of our lives is in direct proportion to our commitment to maintaining quality relationships."
>
> Vince Lombardi

To some extent we have all bought into today's materialism. In all honesty, most of us would think of Donald Trump or Bill Gates before Mother Theresa on the list of those most successful. So how did we get to that point? It's all too easy to cite the news media, the movies, or television, but those are the effects, not the causes. We've actually been conditioned from our earliest years to equate pleasure with *things*; and far too few of us learn as we grow older that things don't even come close to being what's really important in our lives. When (or if) we're lucky enough to reach that point, then we realize that what is important is people. When we don't have people in our lives that *mean* something to us, then the things fail to deliver the good feelings we thought they had promised. The result is an inevitable disillusionment.

We don't have to look very far to see the embodiments of society's notions of success. On the contrary, we're spoon-fed them day in and day out in the form of advertising images — slick, sexy, overdone and hopelessly unattainable. The ads change our notions by touching our senses, and by making us feel that we'll live a better life, be more attractive and be more liked by others if we buy and own things. Again, there's the emphasis on impressing *other people* by spending money. Even with all our years of training in critical thinking, teachers are not immune to the seductive messages society sends us, or to the desire for the material trappings of success. There's certainly nothing wrong with working toward a financial milestone or encouraging our students to do so. What's important is that we not let these influences sidetrack us from our goals.

There's one true part of the message we should be hearing, and that's the emphasis on other people — not on pleasing or impressing them, but on building meaningful connections with them. And for that, we don't need material success at all. In fact, if we could sum up true success in one word, that word would most certainly be "happiness", not "money". If we're not happy in our lives, then we may be many things — rich, powerful, famous — but we're hardly successful because we've failed where it counts the most. When we're teaching our students how to define and pursue their career and monetary goals, we owe it to them to make that abundantly clear.

The same is true for the overwhelming importance of the other people in our lives — something that no school curriculum really emphasizes. As teachers we may teach psychology or the sociology of the family, or safe sex and birth control, but the role others play in our sense of accomplishment and self-worth often goes untaught, or we leave it to be learned in the home or on the streets, for better or for worse. Sometimes we never learn it at all. I myself learned this critical lesson at mid-life when I made an error in judgment that nearly cost me the treasured relationships with people that make my daily successes worthwhile. But those same people gave me permission to fail, and thereby allowed me to get up, repair my damaged self and start to succeed again. That's a wonderful lesson to learn, and it's never too late to learn it.

To accomplish a particular goal, one must first establish *that* goal. To hit the target, that target's got to be present and we have to aim for it. These very simple statements may sum up years of teaching, both in and out of the classroom.

Measuring Success

Throughout this book we've reemphasized several major points:

1. The only people we should be compared to are ourselves, our own inner potential.

2. Satisfaction in life is based on finding something we love doing, and doing it well.

3. To be happy, we need to like the person we see in the mirror every morning.

Now, let me add one more.

4. Success is found in being true to ourselves.

True success is living up to our own standards. What yardstick we use to measure it depends on who we are and what goals we've set — but whether our success marker is a fantastic new software program, a finely crafted cabinet or simply a customer who says "thank you" and sincerely means it, we've succeeded when we've met or exceeded our own standards and been true to our values. What does this mean for teachers? It means that our successes have little to do with the numbers of our students who get into prestigious colleges or win scholarships or awards. They have everything to do with how many of our students find a career that makes them happy and do well in it. If your last graduating class turned out two dozen of the best carpenters, hairdressers or electricians, and they love their work, you should be very proud.

Many students come to us and simply say, "I want to make a lot of money." We smile and nod. Who doesn't, after all… but at what cost? The cliché "money can't buy happiness" may make us cringe, but perhaps that's because we know that it's one of life's most inevitable truths. When a student tells us that he or she just wants a career that will make money, we need to find out why. More often than not, it's because they're unhappy with their life now and want to make sure they can escape it. In that case, we've got to make very sure that they're headed toward a career they will love, because they already know what it's like to hate what they're doing every day. How will they handle hating what they do for the next fifty?

Heading toward a goal that won't make us happy is self-sabotage, or a lifetime spent looking for what does not exist. If we can teach this to our students, chalk up a big marker on our yardstick of success. And what a wonderful success that is!

Who Is a Successful Teacher?

The quickest way to find a successful teacher — the Teacher's Teacher — is to ask other teachers. Who inspires them? Whom do they look to for encouragement? If someone gives you three names, you now know four people who qualify. Similarly, a student can point out the Teacher's Teacher. That's the man or woman they look forward to seeing every day because he or she makes them appreciate that they are worthwhile. That's the man or woman who looks forward to seeing them every day also.

In fact, I'll bet we can all name someone who is or was a successful teacher. That says something very good about us. One of the foremost attributes of a great teacher — the Teacher's Teacher — is the ability to recognize and applaud greatness in our colleagues. When you see that greatness, you must never be afraid to let that person know. At the same time, being a successful teacher also means being part of a successful team, and that means being able to help others improve and grow. Our culture has conditioned us to be quick to point out something that's done wrong, and not necessarily to the person who can do anything about it. We decry or bemoan, but rarely offer truly constructive criticism unless we have something to gain, even if it's only a boost to our own insecure egos. It may not even register with us when something is done very right — or if it does, we may shrink from acknowledging it for fear that it may give that person the right to make demands on us, or give them a competitive edge. But contrary to what you may see around you, *teaching is not a competitive profession.* We are a team, and our goalpost is the common good. We succeed most when we all succeed. So another important marker of the successful teacher is the ability to help other teachers grow and improve — and the ability to take advice in return. How else can we help our students learn to give and accept criticism, in school, at work, and in life?

What about the success factor, though, as society perceives it? A teacher is all the more successful if he or she has a close-knit and supportive family; a comfortable lifestyle; and lots of fond inscriptions in a long series of yearbooks. Can we call a teacher successful who doesn't have these accomplishments? Certainly, but it's a matter of degree. It's always been my core belief that an individual's greatest successes emanate from the strength of the family. That may be the current family of one's life-partner and children; it may be the family in which we grew up, or the family of work, colleagues and friends. Whatever the definition, it's still an essential ingredient of success. Success rings hollow if we have no one to share it with.

My son recently said to me that he felt that ninety percent of his success came from having had a solid foundation with mom and dad, and that he attributes only ten percent of his success to his own efforts. My response to that is, "But aren't those your own efforts?" A successful family is also a team, and we don't rank the players. A successful family is one in which each individual is listened to and respected. True, it's also one in which some of our idiosyncrasies are tolerated. There must always be flexibility also to allow rules to bend instead of break. Our family is the place where we most need to be ourselves.

Maintaining a comfortable lifestyle is largely a matter of common sense. The great teachers convey to their students — that it's a person's self-image that matters, not the world's image of success as a massive collection of *things*.

And what about that wonderful collection of personal messages we have in the cover of our many yearbooks, inscribed on the bottom of the final exam, or in a heartfelt letter received many years later when we least expect it? Add to that the silent testimonials we saw lighting up so many young faces, and we have an amazing number of markers on that yardstick!

Who Is a Successful Student?

Like successful people everywhere, successful students are those who are true to themselves. That certainly does not mean the ones who do as they please, regardless of the rules or the rights of others. It means those who honestly do what's in their own best interest, now and for the future. Successful students understand that they cannot excel in everything. They know that they don't have to be compared to others and that although they are constrained to follow certain requirements for making a contribution to society, they can accomplish that doing something that they love.

It's important for students as well as parents and teachers to understand that their success cannot be defined by what their families or others want for them, even if those people may have the best of intentions. It cannot be defined by numbers on a standardized test. Nor can it be defined by fluency in a certain language, membership in a certain income bracket or an impressive name on a college sweatshirt. Successful students are those who meet their own goals and who choose and follow a path that makes them happy. Successful students are also those who have developed a strong sense of values including respect and self-respect, integrity and caring — values that are always reinforced by the Teacher's Teacher. Above all, these students know that they can change their minds, and that they have permission to fail. Unless one has understood failure, one cannot truly understand success.

When I'm in the private sector, I'm always being told, "Mark, what is most important is the employees' attitude. Are they willing to come to work early? Stay late? Take the extra assignment? Are they willing to walk the extra mile?" Competition is strong, both for jobs and within them. A lot of people out there have good academic credentials and specific marketable skills, so that makes "intangibles" like attitude a key factor in hiring, promotions and success.

Is education important? Yes, it's more important than ever, and I support education for the sake of knowledge. Despite what some modern business theorists and the media may tell us, knowledge for the sake of knowledge *is* important. Everything we learn increases our capabilities, and no type of knowledge is irrelevant or wasted. And yes, students also need to learn about the choices and skills that will help them find a fruitful, happy niche out in the world. Students need to learn the specific skills that allow a person to do his or her job well. That's not to suggest that we should tell students what their fields of study should be, but rather that we need to make sure they understand life's economic necessities and the need to earn their living by succeeding at something that will make them happy. We also need to stress the importance of strong communication skills, which enable people to promote and use their other skills. But most importantly, today young people have got to be aware of building a foundation of skills *and* a strong work ethic. This is something that, too often, people only learn much later through experience. But we can teach it first. Once we've done that, we don't need to be afraid about our students' future.

I see great teachers everywhere, and they are teaching exactly that. What's more, I see the traces of where the great teachers have been, because I see their former students out in the workforce, with the strong characters and successful careers they have built. You can take tremendous pride in them.

A Definition of Success

Now let's finally set the measures of success, for our students and ourselves:

Success is having people in your life who care about you and appreciate what you do.

Success is living up to your own standards.

Success is having clearly defined goals and values.

Success is having balance.

Success is not being afraid or ashamed of the occasional failure that is part of life.

Success is being true to yourself.

Success is knowing you've done the absolute best you can, and feeling proud of yourself for that.

If you are a truly successful individual, then you have allowed yourself to fail and come away from it a stronger and wiser person. Now allow yourself to succeed, and to rejoice and take pride in your success. You have earned that privilege, and all the pride and happiness that go with it. Enjoy!

Chapter 8

Letters from the Real World

Throughout this book, you've heard me talk at length about the power of a positive attitude and the importance of going the extra distance to help students achieve. The goal of this chapter is to show you some examples of those ideas in practice — vivid human stories of caring and perseverance that are so much more powerful than anything I could write. The following letters have been written to me by real people I've met through our public schools — teachers who cared enough to make a difference in a student's life, and students writing about a teacher who helped them get through tough times. They testify to the great things we can do if we try. I call these "letters from the real world" because these students and teachers have lived and breathed what I've been talking about in this book. All references to students have been made anonymous to protect their privacy.

"We were able to save one child"

Mark,

An inspiring experience...I was called to the cafeteria one day when a problem arose when a sophomore student would not move for a teacher. The teacher had asked the student to move to the end of a lunch line for cutting the line. He refused to move. I told him twice to move, and when he refused the second time, I sent him to the office. He refused once again. I approached him and whispered in his ear, "Move or the police will be here, cuff you and take you out." He walked out, proceeded to yell expletives at me and threatened to quit school.

I followed him, took him into an empty wood shop room and talked with him. Mark, he listened, and since then we have had a great relationship. This boy will graduate this year, and I feel we were able to save one child who might otherwise become another statistic.

I will personally hand him his diploma.

Ron Safer, Principal (deceased)
Northbridge High School
Whitinsville, MA 01588

A chance inspiration

It was a warm summer afternoon in July. I sat by an open window at my desk in my ground level principal's office when he poked his head in the window and said, "Hi, Mr. Sals. Remember me?"

Although there was something familiar about him, I must admit that I really did not. His unshaven face, slightly receding hairline and casual appearance kept me in doubt as to his identity.

"I'm C.," he offered, "class of 1987", and I'm home for a few days from Illinois where I'll begin my internship next week at Chicago Hospital."

He went on to say that he had graduated from medical school last month and just had to stop by to thank me for inspiring him to enter the medical profession.

Now I was totally bewildered. How could I have inspired a high school boy who, to the best of my recollection hadn't even been a student of mine, to enter the medical profession? I didn't even teach science. And I told him so.

"Are you sure you're thanking the right person?" I asked.

"I sure am," he responded. "Do you remember the day Mrs. Bartlett, my biology teacher, took sick, and you, in your role as vice-principal, filled in?"

I didn't actually remember, but it was exactly what I did in those days — that is, take the class myself when an unexpected teacher absence arose.

"Well," he continued, "you asked the class what we were studying at the time, and we answered 'genetics'. So you told us the only story you knew about genetics — you know, the one about Mendel and his experiments with the pea pod and his ensuing theory that in a family of four siblings 80% of the time there would be a 3-1 combination — that is, three boys and a girl, or three girls and a boy."

"Yup," I admitted. I've told that story, I recalled, many times.

He continued, "I became so interested in Mendel that I went to the library and did a research paper on him for science class, and it set off in me a genuine interest in the science field which led me to become a biology major in college. I went on to med school and now I'm a doctor. And I owe it all to you and your timely genetics story."

He shook my hand and disappeared as fast as he had arrived. I sat back, basking in what I'd just heard. One never realizes the impact of one's remarks. I certainly didn't.

I wish he would come back so I could tell him what I learned from him.

Bob Salisbury, Principal (retired)
Smithfield High School
Smithfield, RI

"Someone with a future"

I first met H. when I was a teacher in a small public Alternative High School located in a medium sized urban school district. He was not a student — he used to come to school after regular school hours and spend time playing cards, checkers, chess or casually conversing with student friends and members of the staff.

H. was a congenial individual approximately 16 years of age, with quite a sense of humor, although a good deal of his humor was self-deprecating. He would make jokes about his overweight body or his looks or poor posture or his being a school dropout. Sometimes I would broach the subject of his returning to school, and usually he cut that idea short by saying that school was not for him. He would say to me that he didn't have the "smarts" to make it in school.

One afternoon when I was leaving work I noticed a group of students playing poker with H. at a local eatery. I stopped in and watched the game. As an accomplished poker player myself, I was interested in the strategic interchange. What amused me was H. was in control of the game and winning far more than his share of hands. As I watched I saw H. as a very bright person employing strategies that reflected a great deal of intelligence. I also had the opportunity a few days later to observe H. playing chess. What I saw was an analytic mind at work which provided a foundation for strategizing. Needless to say, I was quite impressed with his abilities.

After this I decided to confront him in conversation about returning to school again. After a very long, difficult conversation, he agreed to come in and take a placement test.

When I reviewed the test it was clear what his problem was. H.'s reading level was about second grade, and his writing skills weren't much better. His math skills also tested low, yet one could not discover this from watching him handle money.

H. enrolled in the Alternative School and reported for classes in September with a sense of exuberance and enthusiasm. This enthusiasm, however, began to quickly wear thin when the reality of class work began to set in. Once again the prospect of failure pervaded the process.

Because the Alternative School was built around the concept of personalization, his relationship with the teachers seemed to be the thread that kept him from giving up. Additionally, teachers gave personal time after school to help him with his reading and math. Yet progress was slow and hard, and no matter how hard we tried to build his self-image, it didn't seem to be enough to keep him involved.

At that time I was in charge of the area of medical care studies. This involved a comprehensive study of the U.S. health care system and international approaches, as well as internships in various health care institutions. Even though H. was not eligible under our school rules, the staff decided to make an exception and I asked H. to join the Medical Care Studies area. He reluctantly agreed and came to the Medical Care Seminar, displaying his lack of confidence and his self-deprecating sense of humor. Students in the area had to complete at least one semester in the program before being placed in an internship, but I thought that H. needed an internship as soon as possible. I thought that an internship would expose him to a culture with which he was unfamiliar, namely that of a professional work environment.

I arranged an internship at the local hospital physical therapy department where they would train H. to help lift and transport patients. The patients that H. encountered were paraplegics, quadriplegics and others suffering extreme physical problems: problems that made H.'s problems seem almost insignificant. H.'s personal and good-natured approach soon won him a sense of belonging. Patients depended on him not only for transport but also related to him as a friend, almost like a social worker. H. was someone whom people in great need depended upon. He made them laugh and genuinely cared for them.

This experience had a profound effect on H. Soon he began dressing with a white shirt and tie and began carrying a briefcase. His self-confidence was growing by leaps and bounds, which had a great effect on his school work. He became dedicated to his studies because now he saw himself in a different light. Now he was someone with a future, and the school work was his means to reach success.

H. grew intellectually, his progress was consistent and he was able to graduate at the age of 19. He also won acceptance to a special program at the State University. H. later graduated with a BA in Sociology and went on to receive an MA degree in Business Management at Boston University. H. has become a successful professional member of our community, incidentally earning far in excess of my salary as a public school administrator.

What this shows is that with personalization, proper motivation and a school-to-work experience exposing a student to the professional world of work, anything is possible. A person was able to raise himself against all the odds. This story carries some strong implications for our educational system — namely that if we are to successfully serve students, especially those from the inner city, it is imperative that these students be exposed to the culture of professional work. They have to be in an environment where they no longer see themselves as victims with no viable opportunities for their future, but as capable workers who have value.

Therefore, school-to-work internships are a critical factor in the success equation. The urban school systems must forge a comprehensive relationship with business and professional communities in order to effectively prepare today's youth for the 21st century. This relationship will greatly benefit all parties, because tomorrow's graduates will be prepared to enter the work force as contributors equipped with the tools to be life-long learners, who can make the United States successful and competitive in the 21st century.

Paul Gounaris
Assistant Superintendent of Schools
Professor at Johnson & Wales University
Providence, RI

"D stands for Dad"

This is the story of a young boy who came a long way in four
years. As a ninth grader at Warwick Veterans Memorial High
School, he spent a large percentage of each day in the vice-
principal's office. Anything would set this boy off. He was
kicked out of class for yelling, swearing, being disrespectful to
the teacher, throwing things (desks), and general disruption. The
hallways were another place where he had problems. A wrong
look or a comment from a passing student could be enough fuel
to start a fight.

His home life was in a shambles. Parent conferences were a
waste of time. His mother was convinced he would never
amount to anything, and that it was the school's responsibility to
take care of him during the day. He found out who his real
father was one night when he was 15. There was a man in the
neighborhood that looked like him. The idea of it began to
bother him. Finally, one day he asked the man if they were
related, and he found out the truth. Family members were
spread throughout the Oakland Beach section of Warwick. He
would bounce from one house to another. Often he was seen
lugging his most prized possession, a ratty old sofa bed, up and
down the road. He would crash at his sister's house or maybe at
his grandmother's place. Sometimes he would have to stay with
friends.

There was no end in sight. The problems kept escalating. His
vice-principal, Mr. DiSantis, finally came to the resolution that it
was attention this boy craved. The only way he knew how to get
attention was in a negative way. The inevitable showdown
finally happened. Mr. D. took this boy into his office. He had an
assignment that he had to do, and if he didn't complete it, then
he was going to fail. Mr. D. slammed the door so hard, the clock
fell off the wall. With sparks flying from the wires, Mr. D. gave
his ultimatum: "You have three choices: you do your
assignment, jump out the window, or try to get past me."

This seemed to be the catalyst that began a relationship that would continue through graduation. The next step was to channel some of that energy into positive directions. Mr. D. got him involved with the athletic program. His enormous size and aggressive nature made him a perfect candidate for football and wrestling. Under the guidance of Coach Nappa, he was able to discipline himself and get rewarded with some positive attention. It wasn't all roses though. Trying to keep this boy and his appetite in check was a whole different ballgame.

Mr. D. kept after him through sophomore and junior year. The changes began slowly, but once he settled into a positive routine, the difference was enormous. He joined the community service club at school, and eventually he became the president. His involvement with mentoring elementary students earned him recognition at an awards dinner. On Honors' Night during his senior year he was given the Presidential Award for Educational Effort which was signed by President Clinton. In his four years, he went from a boy who wanted to destroy his community to a young man who wanted to give something back.

During his senior year, it looked like there might be some opportunities beyond high school. With the help of Mr. D., his guidance counselor, and his English teacher, he applied for enrollment at URI through the PEP program which serves disadvantaged youth. He was awarded a full, four-year scholarship. Right now he is in his second year with a 3.2 GPA. His goal is to become a teacher and make Mr. D. proud.

As could be expected, the end of his senior year was an emotional one. He didn't want to leave. This was mainly because school was the only place where he felt wanted, needed, and accepted. There was a lot of hugging. Some of the teachers got together and gave him some necessities that he could take to college with him. He didn't know how to express himself towards his vice-principal who had done so much and had taken him so far. He finally came up with one statement that said it all.

"The D doesn't stand for DiSantis, it stands for Dad."

"A few words of encouragement"

S. was a bright-eyed 15-year-old sophomore who sat in the front row of my English class, seldom participating and doing few of the assignments, her grade bordered on failure. When year's end arrived, she managed to get promoted, and with the exception of a few passing glimpses of her in the hallways, we never again spoke. Before long, S. became one of the hundreds of students that a teacher might forget.

Several years later, I made the decision to leave the teaching profession for that of a high school administrator in a school nearly 50 miles away. I missed the daily interaction with students in the classroom but soon got accustomed to my new role. There are still days when I long for a spirited discussion on the finer points of good composition skills.

Six years after leaving the classroom, I was at an elementary school's recital with my youngest son and my wife. A young lady with a small child approached me. "Do you remember me?", she asked with a smile. It's an often-asked question that rarely gets an honest reply. "You look familiar," I answered while searching my memory. As she held the hand of the young boy at her side, she recounted how she was a poor student who rarely did her work and sat in the front row of my classroom. I now remember the eyes. She told me how she had to quit school when she found herself pregnant.

"When I left school, I studied and passed my G.E.D. I'm now finishing my fourth year of college and plan to be a teacher. You once told me, 'Susan, I don't know why you're doing so poorly, but I can clearly see that you're a bright young lady. Someday you're going to realize how important an education is.' You were the only teacher who ever made me feel good about myself."

I could only smile and thank her for her kind words; we parted as the recital started. I was so proud of what she had accomplished. I thought of how every teacher needed to know that they made a difference.

On the drive home, my wife asked me what kind of student S. was. I replied, "The kind for whom a few words of encouragement made all the difference in the world."

George H. Letendre, Assistant Principal (retired)
Diman Regional Vocational Technical High School
Fall River, MA

"I feel blessed"

In some ways I feel blessed because teaching doesn't feel like a job; it's an activity I go to because I enjoy it. The rewards are the smiles, the hugs, the letters from graduates, the requests to borrow books, the trusting glances and the personal pleas for help. I love the kids! They are wonderfully funny, sad, goofy, and brutally honest. They keep me young and optimistic about the future. I try not to prejudge them, but to size them up by their interaction with me, which has paid off very well.

"You're such a mother," the assistant principal says because I even like the troublemakers who present still more of a challenge to win over, to gain their trust, to connect with in some way. Maybe it is my maternal instinct, but I attempt to understand why they act as they do. What's making them laugh or hurt or lash out? Eventually they learn that I genuinely care and will do what I can to help them. In this way I've cracked a few hard exteriors and would like to think that I've made a difference in their lives. They have all made a significant difference in mine.

Susan Poor, English Department Head
Ponaganset HS
Foster-Glocester, RI

"No one would rescue me...except me"

"I stood at the mirror that morning, bleary-eyed, hung over and shaking. Who was going to come and rescue me? I was thrown out of high school, had been working the local fishing boats, and drinking away my paycheck. My mother was dead and my father wandered the local streets, homeless and unavailable to me. As I looked over my shoulder, I realized no one would rescue me except ME! I called the one person who had always been there for me, my priest, and asked for his help. He got me into AA and suggested I call Cape Cod Regional Technical High School in Harwich and finish my education."

This was the story of a young man who contacted us several years ago to see if we would admit him to one of our technical programs. We did, with some reservations and some strict guidelines. "Dan" (not his real name) met with his counselor twice each month, had weekly group counseling for high-risk students and continued his program with AA. His counselor helped him all the way. Extra help to make up credit was provided, along with weekend support, daily encouragement ... whatever was needed to help Dan succeed — even a place on the American Atlantic Challenge team off the coast of France!

Dan graduated in June 1993 as president of his class with an acceptance and scholarship to the Museum School in Boston. While at Cape Cod Tech, Dan exhibited an extraordinary artistic ability, particularly in sculpture. With the encouragement of his counselor, his shop teacher and a social studies teacher, Dan was introduced to a local artist and apprenticed with him for two years. That experience and two years of masonry primed him for a successful career in art! His first exhibit was at the museum last fall. To this day, one of his first sculptures still hangs in the main office of our school.

Did the support, patience and encouragement provided him at Cape Cod Regional Technical High School make a difference in Dan's life? Just ask Dan the next time he stops by the school to speak to some high-risk teens about not giving up, and about listening to your teachers.

Anonymous
Cape Cod Regional Technical High School

"Never underestimate your positive influence"

Dear Mrs. Matthews,

You may not remember me, but I'll remember you always. I graduated from Charlestown High School in 1981. I am now thirty-three years old.

You were my English teacher for three years at Charlestown High. You tried so hard to teach me! Unfortunately, I had no desire to learn English or any other subject. Instead, I was a nuisance and a class clown. I was frequently absent, and when I did attend class, I was always late. Even when I was sitting in class, I never had any intention of cooperating with you. My thoughts were elsewhere. My primary focus was on getting out of school. I just wanted to hang on the corners and drink alcohol with my friends. Partying was always much more important than school.

At that time, I thought you were a miserable witch, but I realize now that you were the most caring, committed and giving teacher I ever had. You were trying to bring out the best in me and others. If I could turn back the hands of time, I would take advantage of your gift of teaching. I would be the most committed student you would have. My main purpose would be to learn to listen, and listen to learn.

I would like to share with you some of the major changes in my life since high school. My life basically went downhill after I graduated. As a result of continued alcohol abuse, I hit rock bottom at age thirty. I finally had to admit to myself, my family and my friends that I needed treatment for my alcoholism, and I went away to a treatment center in 1992. Since then my life in sobriety has been blessed with many gifts, and one of these gifts is the ability to learn. Currently, I am enrolled in college, majoring in Law.

It is a miracle to me to be where I am today in my life. For many years, I had unsuccessful school experiences. I assumed I was stupid and unable to learn. However, since I became sober, I have been diagnosed with Attention Deficit Hyperactivity

Disorder (ADHD) and a learning disability. I know now that I was not stupid or lazy, but that I had a neurological disorder that went undetected until adulthood. Since I have been on medication for ADHD, education has been a wonderful and pleasurable experience for me.

I consulted with an educational psychologist and she suggested I seek out a tutor. Luckily, I have a friend who is a teacher of students with special needs. She began to tutor me. Her specialty is ADHD and learning disabilities. She taught me strategies, coping mechanisms, and different learning styles. My favorite subject is English.

Mrs. Matthews, I know how difficult it is to be a teacher in the inner-city public school system, especially when students don't appreciate your skills. It took fifteen years after graduation for me to realize what an outstanding teacher you really are! When my professor gave us this assignment to write to a teacher who had an impact on us, I knew immediately in my heart who deserved this recognition. Never underestimate the positive influence you had on students throughout the years.

P.S. Please don't be too harsh on me as you critique my letter-writing skills.

Would you please write back, if possible?

Sincerely,

J.

"The power of a positive attitude"

Four years ago a young lady entered Dartmouth High School from her new foster home in Dartmouth where she would reside with five other foster teenagers. This was the seventh foster home for the teenager in the last four years. This young lady entered school in late September of her freshman year with very low self-esteem and a very poor academic record from her previous school. Within a week, she was acting out and cutting classes, unhappy with her new foster home and the school.

Upon spending some time talking to her, it became clear that she considered herself a throw-away child. Her goal was to get out on the streets as soon as she could and live by her wits.

It became apparent that spending time with her in order to help her develop new lifetime goals, higher self-esteem and a positive lifestyle was essential. At first the student was confused. Why was the principal talking to her every day? Why was someone helping her find a better home, helping her with homework, encouraging her, and even throwing her a first-ever birthday party? After initial resistance, she started to smile, showed her first small successes, had no more discipline problems and began to achieve passing grades.

Her sophomore year started with achievable goals developed by the student herself, in addition to a can-do attitude, better self-esteem and a positive outlook. The year ended with this young lady being involved in student activities for the first time in her school career, and As and Bs for grades which were then proudly shown to her peers and staff. She left for the summer with a smile and a summer job.

Today she is a very involved honor student in her senior year. Also, she is looking forward to going on to a career in social work. Hopefully, she will be teaching others the power of a positive attitude.

Donald King, Principal (retired)
North Dartmouth High School

Setting one's own standards

Dear Mr. Mainella,

On January 7, 1997, you spoke to the senior class of Ipswich High School. You chose me to address by name, and paid me many compliments. This was not the first time I have heard you speak; I was also present as a student mentor when you addressed the freshmen in September. I remembered how you picked people from the audience to speak with personally.

Despite this, I never expected to be one of them when I looked you in the eye as you glanced toward our side of the gym.

One point that had special meaning for me was about not comparing yourself to others. My parents have always wanted me to do better than everyone else in school. Eventually, I wanted this as well, and in some ways I have achieved my goal. Throughout high school, I have ranked number one in the class. But even with this number pinned to my name, I am still compared to high-ranking Ipswich scholars of the past (are the colleges I am looking at as prestigious as those they attend?). I hate this comparison because it means that not only am I competing with my present classmates (which I do not mind), but also with valedictorians from the past. Your words help me remember that I'm the one going to college.

When you asked me whether I knew anyone who really enjoys his or her job (other than teachers), I replied that I did not. Although since then I have thought of a few people who do seem to enjoy working, your point remains valid. I know far more people who do not like their jobs, because they allowed someone else to tell them what field they should pursue. I hope never to be among those people, and I will remember what you said when I have to decide upon a career. As you said, the best surgeon is never looking for work. I have always tried to do my best, despite people who ridiculed me for not believing that an average or slightly above-average effort is adequate. People who believe in doing their best are rare, but they are the ones who can be most satisfied with what they do because they do it well.

Thank you again.

Robin Teague (student)
Ipswich High School
Ipswich, MA

A chance to succeed

Mark, two success stories for you:

K. approached Mr. Kelley to try to convince him that he
should be given an opportunity to attend Norfolk County
Agricultural High School. He had failed sophomore year for the
second time at another high school. He hated school and was
ready to drop out if he couldn't attend the "Aggie." He was
interested in plant science and landscaping, and Mr. Kelley
decided to give him a try.

After three very successful years, K. ended up as valedictorian
of his class. He attended Stockbridge School of Agriculture
where he received his Associates Degree; he then transferred to
U. Mass., completed his Bachelors Degree, and continued his
graduate work in Plant Pathology at Rutgers University. He was
a terrific student and a fine young man.

S. was a very unhappy student at Brockton HS because none
of the classes helped him to learn what he was already doing:
landscaping. He came to the "Aggie" as a junior and was
accepted because of his proven interest in landscape work. He
was completely successful as a student and increased his
business, hiring some of his classmates during their cooperative
work study program. He now runs a very successful landscape
and contracting business.

Clearly, giving students a chance and the encouragement to
be successful is what it's all about.

Ronald A. Cocuzzo and Michael Kelley (retired)
Guidance & Admissions Counselors
Norfolk County Agricultural High School
Walpole, MA

"We can be the catalyst"

Dear Mr. Mainella:

As a school administrator in charge of Student Services, it
amazes me to realize how my path has touched some of today's
youth. Not too many years ago, I encouraged a quiet and
somewhat shy young man, in his sophomore year in my High

School, to accompany me and some other students to speak to eighth graders within the local school community, about the merits of a vocational technical education. With some encouragement he did fine. As we ventured out into other schools to make a presentation his confidence seemed to grow as did his enthusiasm.

After eight or nine presentations, he really projected such wit and self confidence that I felt he had grown into an articulate young man with determination and style. His grades seemed to improve and he ran for office and became president of his class. He was also involved in our radio station at the school.

Unbeknownst to me, he had a situation with an instructor that began to get the best of him. He felt really put down by this instructor to a point where he wanted to leave the vocational technical school or quit school all together. When he approached me with a note from home to transfer, I brought him into my office. I told him that I was not going to let him transfer in order to escape from a situation that could be resolved. It was well over an hour later that he finally agreed to let me intervene on his behalf. I explained this to his parents.

Two years later, he graduated with top honors, and became our first vocational technical student to be honored at an awards assembly as Outstanding Vocational Secondary student. Upon graduation he opened his own electronics business on the east coast, then opened another office on the west coast. Since that time he has ventured into other areas, and at this writing has over 50 people working for him and is making a six-figure income. We still keep in touch.

I hope this experience helps others to realize how important it is to reach out to students. It can really make a difference in their lives. Every individual has the potential to be whatever they want to be, to achieve whatever they want to achieve, if they only realize their own self-worth. We can be the catalyst that could make that happen in the lives of others, by being there for them, giving them that encouragement and lending them a firm hand when needed. Our path crosses many lives. We can make a difference, if we take the time to help others see that they have a special gift within, a special talent that needs to be nourished and nurtured. Nothing is impossible if you see it, imagine it and believe it.

Mr. Benjamin Monfredo (retired)
Director of Pupil Personnel Services
Bay Path Regional Vocational Technical High School
Charlton, MA

Triumph over tragedy

Two years ago, a young lady from Stafford High School was involved in an auto accident. She was a passenger in the back seat with her seatbelt on (the older version that just went around the waist). The car slid on some ice at a moderate speed and hit a tree. A., the young lady, had her spinal cord broken (the impact doubled her over). She was the only person injured.

She went from a talented athlete to a paraplegic. Although involved in athletics, A. had been otherwise quiet and not active in other school programs. She was a hard worker, but her grades weren't exceptional.

Before the accident, I barely knew A. After the accident, everyone knew A. — but not because of her injuries. She clearly had strength and courage which were not seen prior to her accident. She refocused her life in new directions. No longer able to compete in athletics, she became the most active and successful student council president I had ever seen in my eleven years at Stafford. From here she volunteered to use experimental leg braces being developed at Newington Children's Hospital. Her progress was documented by the local CBS television affiliate WFSB Channel 3 in Hartford. The television documentary attracted the attention of U.S. House of Representatives member Sam Gejdenson who invited her to meet the President as he got off his plane in New London.

A.'s goal was to walk (with braces) to her junior prom. She walked to the prom on braces she had helped perfect, and when she was selected prom queen, she was featured on the six o'clock news. A. later became president of her senior class and is scheduled to attend college in the fall of 1997.

This is an account of someone who overcame great personal tragedy to succeed in other areas of her life. A. is probably a stronger and in many ways more capable person as a result.

Dr. David Perry, Principal (retired)
North Branford High School
North Branford, CT

Positive action

Mark,

I was once asked which subject was my favorite to teach to my second graders. After thinking about this for a minute or two, I realized that the subject that I enjoy teaching my students is not math, or science or social studies. My favorite subject is teaching the children to feel good about themselves, to love themselves and to respect each other.

During the course of the school year I want my second graders to work cooperatively in groups while reading books, performing science experiments and engaging in several other activities. In order for them to be able to do this, I realize that I must first teach them how to work together and how to get along with one another.

I have adopted and augmented a program called Positive Action (developed by Carol Gerber Allred, Ph.D.) to which I was first introduced while working as an elementary school teacher in the Yonkers Public Schools. I start off with Positive Action on the first day of school, and the program is continued throughout the year up until the very last day of school.

The year starts with the children learning about the positive actions that will keep themselves in a positive frame of mind.

They learn phases like "self-concept" and "self-esteem," and they learn the differences between positive and negative actions as well as the effects that these actions can have. When it comes time to discipline a student, I am able to use this vocabulary and I can ask, "Was that a positive or negative action? How did your actions affect the other child's self-concept?"

As the year progresses, we learn about positive actions which will keep our bodies healthy, such as eating healthy foods, getting enough rest and exercising. The children then learn about social positive actions such as helping, sharing and caring for one another. Much of this is done through storytelling, classroom meetings and role play. The students in my class learn to treat each other with kindness and respect.

Mental positive actions come next. These are positive actions that will keep our minds healthy, such as being curious and asking good questions, and being resourceful and creative. We learn that it is important to exercise our minds as well as our bodies.

By learning about positive actions throughout the entire year, my second graders become confident people who are not afraid or embarrassed to experiment and try new things. They treat each other fairly and with respect, and they feel comfortable expressing themselves because they know that they will be supported not only by their teacher, but by their classmates as well.

The many activities that go on in my second grade classroom would not be nearly as successful as they are if I did not first stress the importance of using positive actions right from the first day of school. I love to watch my students grow into young people who are sure of themselves, and Positive Action is my favorite subject to teach.

Mitchell Crasson, Elementary school teacher
Scarsdale, NY

"A little kindness and attention"

She was 15, plump, lacked esteem, and underachieved. Paradoxically, she was a descendant of one of the oldest and richest families in town. Seemingly then, she had the stuff to have a fun-filled, successful youth, but — S. was a mess.

I was teaching ninth grade English in those days, and had her report to me after school one day for a lack of homework and general academic listlessness. It was the start of a memorable experience.

S. "wore" an unpleasant smell, not unlike the combination of pot, stale alcohol, and body odor. After covering my criticisms she asked if we could discuss more serious matters - more serious than academic failure? And would I agree to confidentiality? Well! The principle of double effect kicked in, so I promised.

She pushed up the sleeves of her ever-present black sweater and there on her dirt-encrusted wrists were the scars of some old razor cuts — not deep enough to cut into the vein. It was perhaps the premeditated start for a girl so unhappy with herself that she wanted to end it.

What to do? Help her experience some success!

She was in my daily study hall so I started working on her missing assignments. We talked about the essay due, the book report, the quiz. It was nothing as magical as an elixir, but after the first week her demeanor changed. There was a bounce to her walk and she wore an occasional smile. When she came into the study the next week with her homework and drafts of the assigned report and essay, I knew there was hope for this girl.

What a little kindness and attention can do is inestimable! As the weeks went by, she became more animated in class and began speaking to other students. The metamorphosis had started when she came to school one day with a change of clothing and a scent of soap. Again, a little attention paid such enormous results — a person's life, perhaps.

Some years later I was interviewing for an English teacher opening. A well-dressed, attractive and intelligent woman walked into my office. After the interview, S. left no doubt in either of our minds that the job was here.

The metamorphosis was complete!

Anthony J. DeMeo, Assistant Principal (retired)
Barrington Middle School
Barrington, RI

Touching the future

Dear Mr. Mark Mainella:

Many of my friends have jobs that pay much more than I make, but none of these people can ever experience the joy, sense of accomplishment and fulfillment when a young person returns after years to see me in my office and says thanks for caring, thanks for being there for me whenever I needed help and support. As a Guidance Counselor, I can truly say that I "touch the future" when I help a student be successful in life. Nothing can ever replace this feeling and my position as a Guidance Counselor at Warren Harding High School in Bridgeport, CT allows me to experience many of these situations.

One experience that comes to mind is about a young lady who graduated from Harding in June of 1996. She had always been absent and tardy to school many times over the years. She had repeated the sophomore year because of her absences. Her grades were just passing and she always talked about quitting school because she felt that school was not going to help her. When this young lady was a freshman we first met and as the days passed we continued to meet more frequently and we got to know each other quite well. We always discussed how important it was for her to finish and graduate from high school and to help her succeed we changed some of her classes along the way. We changed some of her teachers and very importantly we gave her some responsibilities as a clerical intern in the main office for one period a day during her junior years and her senior years. During these high school years she also became involved in a negative relationship with a young man who was suicidal. I always had time for her, but knowing how important her boyfriend was I began seeing them together, trying to help their relationship, but more importantly trying to reach this young man to offer him help and support.

I tell my students when I first meet them that if they feel comfortable with me being their Guidance Counselor then I will always be their Guidance Counselor. Always, meaning while they are at Harding and afterwards as well. Presently, even though this young lady has graduated I still talk to her on the telephone and at times she even stops in to see me. In September 1997 she came to see me and let me know things were going all right, but she had stopped working because the store closed down. She informed me that she filled out an application for a position through a labor force organization. Immediately I contacted this company and spoke to the Director of Personnel about my student, explaining to him how I watched this young lady grow and mature into a responsible young lady over the years. Two days later this young lady was hired by the company and as I write this story on 1-6-98, she is doing well at this position.

As a Guidance Counselor I know teenagers need people in their corners who care. I want to be in as many corners for teenagers as possible today. I enjoy and respect my position as a Guidance Counselor at an inner city high school like Harding because it enables me to make a difference in people's lives.

Joseph DeVellis, Guidance Coordinator
Warren Harding High School

"The Best Lesson to Students is your Own"
Mr. M,
I am humbled to hear that you refer to yourself as not a smart man. I disagree! My dear sir, you are a genius, your intensity, your dedication to speaking to students in the manner you do

will stay with them. The best lesson to students is your own
story. Everyone can find something in you to relate to you. This
makes a difference. And for that I thank you. Please continue
what you are doing. The lessons you talk about, soul in the eyes,
is something they will reflect upon. You are in control of your
destiny and what an amazing thing to you have chosen to do.

All my best,
Melissa Gerry

"My Story goes Full Circle"
Hi, my name is Barbara Michello, and I work as a
paraprofessional at Classical High School in Lynn
Massachusetts. One day in 2005, shortly after the start of the
school year, the freshmen class was scheduled to attend an
assembly. As I sat in the auditorium, listening to our guest
speaker, my first inward response was shock. This man who
stood speaking before us was nothing like I had ever seen or
heard before. He was very blunt, somewhat rude, and didn't
soften his tone at any point in time to the audience. However, he
had my undivided attention as he spoke of the importance of self
respect and the respect for the people around you. This was the
key to the quality of life; if you wanted to be accepted in society
today. I was raised with respect, taught my children respect, and
it will always be an important part of my life. It felt good to hear
Mr. Mainella bluntly telling this to the freshmen class; especially
the ones who needed to hear it. They need to smarten up, get the
chip off their shoulder, and choose a goal and work hard to
achieve it in their life before it was too late. Too late meant after
learning a lesson the hard way, like going to jail, dropping out of
school and not being accepted into the community in which you
live. As my shock began to fade, I started to realize which part of
the audience he was addressing. He was addressing the students
that had no respect for them or anyone else and them only way
to get them to listen was to talk to them the way they talk,

because in the real world that is how it is. Blunt and painfully true, no one was going to baby them their whole lives and the sooner they realized that the better off they were. I found myself enjoying the lecture the more Mr. Mainella spoke. As he continued, I suddenly felt something familiar to me in what he was saying. I remembered a conversation I had with my youngest daughter Colleen, who had graduated from Classical in 2005. She had come home from school and told me she had an assembly and how embarrassed because when Mr. Mainella asked the question, "how many of you have parents that like their job", my daughter was the only person in the auditorium that had raised her hand. My heart melted and I smiled, but it felt strange to have to explain that it was nothing to be ashamed or embarrassed about to have been the only person to have her hand raised. In fact, to me it was rather sad, but on the same note, I felt as though I had to defend myself and my actions as a parent. I asked her to consider what kind of home life some other kids went home to every day. People who don't like their jobs are usually miserable. If they had a bad day, they as a rule come home and take it out on the people they love most. Therefore, making life for everyone in the house horrible. There could be fighting, drinking, and anger on a daily basis. No one should have to live their life like that. That is the voice of experience talking, you see, years ago I chose to change how miserable we were by getting a divorce because I didn't want us to have to live like that. She should be proud and happy to not have to worry about what kind of day I had or wonder what kind of mood I would be in on any given day. We were lucky to have a "normal" routine with very few upsets. I will admit that this conversation was not one I thought that I would have with anyone, especially one of my children. It is true in life that some things are taken for granted, but I didn't think one's own home life was one of them. At the end of our conversation she confessed that she was still embarrassed, but agreed she was indeed lucky.

When Mr. Mainella had finished his presentation, I couldn't help but introduce myself to him and tell him my story. He gave me a starfish pin, thanking me for sharing my story with him, and for having such a good relationship with my daughter, because she came home and told me about her day at school.

My story goes full circle; I went home and thanked my daughter for the pin. She had a very confused look on her face, but after I told her about the assembly I went to that day, we both smiled. It is the best piece of jewelry I could ever/will ever have. There is no monetary value that could ever take the place of my starfish. I wear it faithfully every day, and I am proud to have it.

I would like to thank you for taking the time to ready my story and experience. I am grateful that to have had the opportunity to share it with you. However, I am the lucky one, I have two great daughters that I am very proud of, for different reasons, but they both come back to respect and what the starfish represents.

Barbara Minchello, paraprofessional
Lynn Classical High School

Chapter 9

Examples of Excellence

I was told when I started out that my vision of reaching students through public speaking was impossible. No one, I was told, will allow you to take class time to talk about generalities like careers, goal-setting, self-image. But what has become apparent to me is that if I can bring value for the student into the classroom, teachers who truly care not just about academic performance but about the whole person will gladly share their class time. Teachers who understand that academic performance is founded on self-respect and a sense of personal motivation welcome this opportunity, because I reinforce for the student the values that great teachers teach every day. In the long run, I don't take time away from the teacher or the class—I help make the students better partners in their own education. Teachers say to me all the time that their kids are more manageable, more willing to listen, more polite, more respectful, when you give them a sense of their own personal value.

Throughout this book, you've been hearing about remarkable teachers I've met while doing exactly that. In this brief chapter, I am going to spend some time talking about just a few more: a handful of special people who stand out in my mind as models of commitment and effectiveness in our schools. These are people who have demonstrated in numerous ways that they will do whatever it takes to enable their students to do the very best they can do, in whatever mode of life they choose. These teachers don't distinguish between "good" students and "bad" students, between college prep students and business track students—they don't see stereotypes. Instead they look at each individual to find the best that exists within his or her being.

These aren't just great teachers, they are great leaders. As principals or assistant principals or headmasters, they set the tone for the teachers who work with them. They make it clear that they demand the best from teachers as from students, and they inspire everyone around them to achieve that goal. And they do this in situations that others have pronounced hopeless—in the biggest, toughest, most "troubled" school systems in New England. Time and time again, I have been warned away from visiting schools like these, by people who fear that in an assembly with hundreds of kids from lower-income areas, discipline would get out of hand. And time and time again, I have seen the true leadership and character of the principals of these schools, as they create an atmosphere of respect and high expectations, where students feel good enough about themselves that they don't need to act out or draw attention to themselves. They have pride in themselves and in their school, because they see their principal has pride in them. I have never had a problem in these schools.

The handful of people in this chapter have my highest respect and affection. I've been honored to know them, and I hope through their example I can show you what the Teacher's Teacher really is.

Mary-Ann and Larry Mathews

Mary-Ann Mathews is one of the first people I met who demonstrated again and again that for her, the student always comes first. In 1978 the busing crisis in Boston was at its peak, beyond what words can describe: not only in South Boston but at many other Boston area schools, Charlestown in particular. Townies did not want their sovereign turf invaded by blacks, end of story. Hers is a school of great sports tradition, predominantly Irish, and when I met Mary-Ann she said, "Mark, if you can't complement my students, if you can't help them to be the best they can be, I'll personally see to it that you never work in this school again." She was a tough little Irish girl. In those days, besides assemblies, I was doing one-period programs class by class through the English department. During one of these presentations, I heard noise outside the room. I walked to the door, looked out into the corridor, and saw an incredible scene. There were people fighting in every square inch of the hall, on every floor: the school had erupted into violent confrontation between the various groups.

I knew that Mary-Ann cared about students, but what happened at that moment blew me away. She had been knocked down onto the floor in the melee. I stopped the lecture and rushed out, picked her up and urged her to get out of there. I'm a tough guy, but I wanted to escape. There were police surrounding the building, and no one could get in or out. Things were looking pretty bad. But she said to me, "No, Mark, they're good kids. You don't understand—you've got to help them." And she and the other teachers went out in the hallways, calming down the students, restoring order. I was thinking to myself, no one is going to even believe this. Ten minutes later, the kids were back in the classroom, I was back in the lecture. When the period was over, I saw Mary-Ann and told her it was unbelievable. She said to me, "No, but what it takes is a commitment to making a difference. We've got some great teachers here who really care about kids." It was characteristic of her to give the credit to the other teachers, but in fact if she hadn't cared so much and set the example by her leadership, the situation would have been much worse. One of her great qualities is that she doesn't see herself for the hero she is.

A couple of years later I met her husband, Larry Mathews, who teaches in the same building and also coaches basketball. I saw him shaking hands with all the students coming into his class. When I asked him about it, his response was "Mark, it only takes a fraction of s second to let every one of my students know that I know they're in class, that I care they're in class, and that I want them to succeed." Mary-Ann told me the same thing. She learned early on that if students believe you care — if they know you want them to succeed — their attention will improve and their attendance will improve. In that school, as with many inner city schools, absenteeism is a huge problem. Larry and Mary-Ann had a higher percentage of students coming to class simply because the students knew that these teachers truly cared about them. And that was the first step.

More stories about Larry and Mary-Ann appear in the Pulitzer Prize-winning book *Common Ground: The Definitive Story of Boston Busing*, which was also made into a movie. Larry and Mary-Ann are portrayed by actors. I remember laughing at one point with Larry because there was a question as to whether he would be played by Paul Newman or Robert Redford — in the end, it turned out to be a relatively unknown actor who did an excellent job portraying what the Teacher's Teacher is all about. Twenty-eight years later I'm still working with Larry and Mary-Ann, and they are as dedicated as ever.

Verna Lauria (retired)

I met Verna in the mid-1980s when she was working as an Assistant Principal for Guidance in New York City, at the William E. Grady Technical School in Brooklyn. It was immediately apparent that for her, the students came first. On this particular day I had had a great session in the auditorium with the kids. It was late in the day and I had offered to take her to lunch as a token of thanks and to share some personal thoughts away form the business of the school. We were just walking out of the building when a secretary said "Miss Lauria, one of your students' parents is here to see you." No appointment, no forewarning. We looked at each other and smiled; I knew right away that there was no question what she would do. I got to work on the phone as usual, while Verna got into a conversation, a difficult one: the student's mother had

traveled by subway all the way from the Bronx through
Manhattan into Queens, across Brooklyn, not knowing that you
can't just show up and expect to see the head of Guidance
without any advance warning. She also barely spoke English,
but it was apparent to Verna that this woman was desperately
trying to keep her daughter in school. Her feelings were no
different from a mother or father in Greenwich or Grosse Pointe,
and Verna didn't treat her differently. This mother made it clear
that she was willing to do whatever it took to keep her daughter
in school, but she was looking for help from the school, and in
particular from Verna as head of Guidance.

An hour and a half later, we left the building, heading for
now a very late lunch. I asked Verna whether this happened
often. "Yes," she replied, but then added, "Mark, I work with
kids who have great, massive needs, and often there is very little
support from families, In this case, I had to spend the time with
this mother, whether or not she had an appointment: she got to
me. Just looking in her eyes it was apparent that she truly was
reaching out for someone to help her to help her daughter." And
that's the way Verna works, every day; there was no way she
would walk away from an opportunity to help.

Les Correia (deceased)

I met Les Correia as an assistant principal at Hartford High. I
had been told to stay out of the school by other school districts in
the area, simply because it was such a tough school. When I
called him up, the first thing he said to me was "What have you
got for my students?" He didn't ask my name, he wasn't
concerned with the color of my skin or my ethnic
background—just with how I could help his students. I
explained what I do, reinforcing values and teaching self-
respect. He said immediately, "You're not going to work with
my seniors— before we even think of seniors, I want you to hit
my freshman with attitude, respect and responsibility. We'll do

it as a test: they're the most difficult group." Now, in general I tend to avoid working with freshmen because of the maturity level, and because of the expectations people bring to the situation. After all, we're talking about 500 ninth graders in the auditorium for something like two hours. I've learned again and again that I'm only as good with my audience as the people who bring me in allow me to be. I had also heard some nasty things about this school. But when we started the session, I watched Les's presence, and I heard his proclamation to the students: "We are Hartford High, we're as good as any school in America. I expect you to act like mature, respectful human beings. Don't one of you even think of embarrassing me by acting like a fool." For the next ninety minutes I didn't have to stop once. The respect Les had earned from his students was transferred to me. He's the Teacher's Teacher. The kids knew he cared.

Ev Waylans and John Getz (retired)

I first met John Getz and Ev Waylans in the 1980s, when John was at Platt High School in Meriden, Connecticut, and Ev was teaching at Danbury High School, Connecticut's largest high school. Ev is now the Assistant Principal at Danbury, and John is the Principal, but at the time I was dealing with a different administrator. I had been trying to get an opportunity to do a session at the school for a long time, and had been told that the school was simply too big: they couldn't control a group the size we'd need to have. However, when John came in as the new Principal, and when Ev took the time to investigate the kind of presentation I do, they accepted my proposal to work with their seniors.

The result was an absolutely fabulous session. The very next year, after some great discussion with John and Ev, we decided for the first time ever in school history to try a ninth-grade assembly. John introduced Ev, and set the tone by telling the students that he had great expectations of their ability to act like

mature adults, and of their future potential for success. Ev then
introduced me, telling the students emphatically how much the
administrators, faculty, and staff at DHS cared about them, both
in the mass and individually. He said that day, "We want every
one of you to succeed. We're doing something we don't
normally do, that many schools never do. We're doing it because
we believe you can handle the truth. Mr. Mainella is here to
share the truth: you can do it." The students applauded, and we
had an absolutely fabulous session without a single problem.
The rest is history: at Danbury High School we now have
sessions for all the seniors, for all the ninth-graders. But my
success depends on the great people there: they care about kids.

Don Pellegrini (retired)

At age 28, Don Pellegrini was the youngest headmaster to take
over a Boston high school in the history of Boston schools, and
he is still there today. I've seen students search out Mr. Pellegrini
to get him to write something nice in their yearbook, saying in
effect "Mr. P., you cared — you made a difference for me at West
Roxbury High School." West Roxbury is a very difficult school
with a diverse student body, predominantly black and Hispanic.
Don Pellegrini has earned a reputation as a stern disciplinarian,
but utterly fair and caring. Again and again, I've seen him
interact with students and staff doing things that many would be
afraid to do. He would always position himself where the
student came first, and everybody knew it—and that's the secret
to the success he has experienced at West Roxbury.

Mike Donato (retired)

Mike took over a most troubled school, Hyde Park, in the late
1970s. When I expressed concern about working in the school,
Jean Moreli said to me, "Mark, we have a principal here who
cares about the kids. You're not going to have any problems

with our students." And of course Jean herself cared deeply. Mike's story is also documented in *Common Ground*. He turned around a school that was in chaos, and brought order to the school by infusing both his faculty and his students with a strong sense of taking responsibility for one's own actions.

Mike Longo (retired)

When I met Mike Longo he was an Assistant House Master at New Bedford High School, one of the largest schools in New England with over 3000 students. He demonstrated character, commitment, and a passion for making a difference for his students, and he ultimately worked his way to House Master, then to Headmaster, then became Assistant Superintendent, and now is the Superintendent of New Bedford Public Schools. I was told back in 1977 to stay out of New Bedford High School; they had just had a riot outside the building and it was a risky place to work. But since that time I've watched for 28 years while teachers, support staff, and administrators across the board proclaim, "We are family!" This may sound trite, but I had an opportunity to see just what it meant some years ago. I had just finished a lecture at New Bedford High School, and a young lady approached to thank me. The headmaster at the time, Joe Oliver, spotted this young lady amidst all the post-lecture confusion and asked what she had said. I asked him why he was curious. He responded that the previous night it had been on the news that her mother had cut her live-in boyfriend into pieces. I asked him in horror what the kid was doing in school, and I'll never forget his reply. "Mark," he said, "don't you get it? We are the best part of many of our students' day. They live amid chaos and turmoil. She was in my office at 6:30 this morning. Police are in her house, news cameras everywhere: the best place she could find to be was the high school. She knocked on my door and I was there."

Cornelia Kelley (retired)

Cornelia Kelley is the headmaster of Boston Latin High School, the most elite public school in America. I've been visiting Boston Latin for 28 years, working with former headmasters and now with Cornelia. She has demonstrated a unique approach by not only using me with her students (the so-called academic elite, the ones who tested at the top of the 100,000 students in Boston), but also with her teachers.

Her message was that her students aren't better — perhaps they're more academically disposed, but they still need to know the value of respect and common courtesy. They need to know that many people as bright as they may still fall into a career they hate, or experience a less than rewarding life, simply because someone told them that because they're so smart they should be a doctor or a lawyer. Actually, everyone has some unique strength that deserves to be developed. She said to me, "I want them to hear about the reality of the working world — the need to find a niche where you fit."

Her students are always being told they're better because they're gifted academically, and her faculty are told they're the best as well. But she wants her teachers to be able to connect with all students. She wants her teachers to give their all to every student, every shape and size and disposition. She wants the Teacher's Teacher on her staff, the one who can motivate all students on any level.

This is profound and significant coming from her. She's positioned to be an academic elitist, but on the contrary, she is teaching humility and constant striving. What she says is that she has great kids and great faculty, and every day she challenges them not to be complacent, not to take anything for granted, but to work to be the best they can be.

Bernard Gassaway

Bernard Gassaway is the former principal of Beach Channel High School in Queens, New York. He left Beach Channel High School because he was outraged by an incident between a student and a teacher, in which he felt the teacher was in the wrong. He put his career on the line standing up for the student, saying that if the teacher were not removed, he himself would resign. The teacher's union defended the teacher and Bernard left, without a clear sense of where his career was headed. But as it turned out, with a new educational regime in New York City, he found another niche and has become the Superintendent of Alternative Learning Programs for the city, overseeing some forty different programs all over the five boroughs.

Although I've been told to stay out of the inner city schools, Bernard has been instrumental at getting me into these so-called at risk school programs, and giving me opportunities to meet the students who fill them and the teachers who work there. I have seen first-hand how teachers in these programs work every day to help and inspire the kids who need it the most. Bernard Gassaway creates the climate where these teachers can do their best. He sets the bar as high for his faculty and students as anyone in any system, in hardcore inner city settings.

And a few more...

I want to close this chapter by talking briefly about three special examples who come to mind, exemplary teachers from these programs who have made a special difference. Ms. Etel Elman worked under Bernard Gassaway's auspices at the Manhattan Learning Center, and has finally retired after a career spent working with these kids. The standard view of these schools is that their students somehow can't, or won't, or don't want to achieve anything. But the truth is that for many of the kids in these special programs, this is the first time in their lives that they've encountered teachers who believe in them, who tell them "you can", not "you should give up." Talking to teachers like Etel, you hear of kids who are going back to school after dropping out, working nights, getting their GED. And they say "Etel told me I could amount to something." She gave them something to work towards, and the confidence in themselves that they needed to persevere.

Another great example is Frank Dody, principal of Island Academy, the high school for prisoners at Rikers Island. He chose to teach there, moving to this program from a job at a suburban high school on Long Island. He is helping to give the inmates a chance to come out with a new start, with the basic skills and education to pursue a life that's not a dead end. And finally, Eileen Taylor, principal at the High School of Aviation Technology in Queens, knows from experience that high school can be enough to launch a productive life, if it teaches the skills and the attitude kids need to succeed. When she took over Aviation Technology, she said to me that if she were to pull her graduates out of LaGuardia, Newark, and Kennedy, she could stop air traffic in New York. She wasn't boasting: she was just pointing out that you don't need to go to college to have a good career, as long as you learn the work ethic and the drive to excel at whatever you do.

Chapter 10

A Plan for Action

All of you who have come with me this far have one thing in common: you're goal-oriented. Therefore, what we need now is a plan for action. Of course, there will be many plans, because beyond this basic fact we're a very diverse group, and we're heading in many different directions. There will be action for those who will remain in teaching, and for those who won't. There will be action for those completing their careers, and for those just starting. There will be action for those who have found their commitment to excellence, and action for those still waiting for that thrill to happen. Understand one thing clearly, though: no plan is *better* than another — just better suited to the individual implementing it — and that makes all the difference.

Losing the Fear

Amid all the challenges a teacher faces in the classroom, fear is the greatest obstacle. And generally speaking, I find that people are fearful. They're forever asking, "If I lose this job, what's available to me elsewhere? What will I do? Can I make it in a new endeavor? Can I make it in this one? What if I'm defeated or humiliated? What if I fail?"

That fear inhibits our own true potential for excellence because we never know how far we can go if we step beyond our comfort zone. For example, in truth there are teachers who would rather not be teachers, but they stay in the game because they're afraid of not being able to make it in the private sector.

Others are truly dedicated to the teaching profession but they defeat themselves through their fear of not measuring up. Some are afraid of the tremendous power that teachers have to mold or direct people's lives. After all, next to our parents, teachers are perhaps the most influential people in our lives. A child can't pick his teachers; and for the most part he can't control how he reacts to them, especially in the younger years, so that influence must be a powerful one indeed. Such an awesome responsibility can be a powerful source of fear. What if they give the wrong direction? What if they cause someone harm? And so many are afraid they will fall short of the expectations of their most constant and unrelenting critic: themselves.

Much of our fear comes from the filter through which we view our current experience as adults. We've all been students, and we all have vivid memories, both good and bad. It's naive to think that those memories don't influence our perceptions and our behavior as teachers. One of my most powerful recollections is of teachers who told me — quite literally — that I was "a big dumbbell" and "not going to amount to much." I can still hear the echoes of that teacher who told me I should quit school because I was wasting both my and her time. I was 12 years old. I internalized that message deeply, and it took years to get myself out of the negative mindset that I just didn't have what it takes. After that, I faced my own fear, and I succeeded in conquering it. I wonder where that teacher is today. Has she succeeded in conquering hers?

To a child, the teacher has all the answers; the teacher is all-knowing. So when a teacher, with such power of presence in the classroom, uses that power to break character, to destroy the spirit, the results can be staggering, and that is something to fear. But should you let that fear cripple you? No, indeed! If you have come with me this far, then you are at the opposite end of the spectrum. You are a dedicated, caring teacher whose goal it is to make sure that situations like this don't happen. You are the one who builds confidence and character as well as instills learning. You help students internalize their own self-worth. No, you can't protect every student from life's inevitable trials and even its inevitable injustices, but you can imbue them with life's strongest weapon against these harmful influences: self-confidence and self-respect, along with a healthy sense of how they can direct their own destiny.

Here's a truly frightening story a friend shared with me. When she was in second grade, her teacher made her crawl under her desk and told her that if she didn't stop talking then the teacher would press a button that would send the little girl to hell. I asked my friend how long the teacher kept her under the desk, and she smiled and said, "Mark, I was there all day."

We all know that there are people in the teaching business who don't belong there. Some have the fear that comes with insecurity: they don't like themselves, they don't like what they're doing, and most of all they don't like kids. You will come across these people, and at first they may frighten you as much as they frighten your students. There are also those who have a more subtle kind of fear, masked by overconfidence. They feel they have nothing to learn, no need to keep growing as teachers. Once, in an in-service, a man said to me, "I'm 49 years old. I've been to hell and back, I'm a Vietnam vet, and no one's going to tell me how to be a better teacher." Indeed there is a very small percentage of teachers who believe that they already are as good as they can be, and that they have all the answers. Like the woman who made an obscene gesture at the in-service, they may be all too eager to say so. However, aren't these few spoilers the most fearful of all? They aren't willing to stay or to listen or to discuss or to learn because they're afraid of being proved wrong.

There isn't much we can do to obviate that kind of fear, because at some point they *will* be proved wrong, as will all the rest of us. Having unrealistic expectations doesn't eliminate fear, it amplifies it, and with good reason. Understand, though, that these teachers are the rare exceptions. At every school I visit, my experience has been that about 80 to 90 percent of the faculties tell me they love teaching. And you *can* help to undo the damage done. What we all can do is lose the fear that's holding us back from our commitment to excellence. We can have the greatest respect for ourselves and for our students and our colleagues, and we can show it. We can shake their hands, and maintain eye contact. We can connect. We can make them understand that we care. We can succeed and succeed, and yes, we can fail. But at that point, we say, "I missed the mark? I failed? Good, because now I can brush myself off and get back to work. My students are waiting."

Together let's help the people who want to connect with the kids — the loving, caring, sharing teachers who help build character, help youngsters succeed, and help them to commit to being the best they can be. Let's also try to help those who hate what they're doing move into another arena. *They're there because of fear.* It's their own negative self-image and their perceived notion of perpetual failure that are keeping them there, and we can help them to see that and move on to a different path to success.

We lose our fear when we help others, and we lose our fear when we see the overwhelming good in our students and in ourselves. Always see this clearly, and you'll never have to face that fear again.

Committing to Excellence

Just getting by from day to day is no way to live. Regardless of whether you like your job or you don't, your short-term goal must be a commitment to doing the best that you can do at it. However, your long-term goal must be to find what makes you happy.

Teaching is one of the world's most rewarding professions, but no profession is rewarding to someone who dislikes what he or she is doing every day. Three out of four adults hate their jobs, and that sets a bad enough standard for our young people. Moreover, making professional martyrdom an example is not doing your students a favor. *It's no disgrace* to say that you might have made a mistake in your choice of career — rather, owning up to that shows wisdom and maturity, a precedent your students will do very well to follow. If you truly do not love teaching, then look till you find where it is that you truly belong. In so doing, you will be teaching your students one of the most valuable lessons they can learn.

When you find something you really love doing, then there's no problem with committing to excellence. If you love it, you work at it with more commitment, and the better you get, the more you enjoy what you're doing. So, committing to excellence is all tied into finding something you love doing. It's an upward spiral with an endless reward of success.

When teaching is what you love, then that reward is immense and timeless. Of course, a commitment to excellence also means a commitment to ourselves. Yes, that means knowing how to recognize and try harder when we fall short; but it also means giving ourselves credit and taking pride when we know we've done well. The world, and especially the world of work and of education, is always quick to point out when things don't meet its preconceived notions, and rarely points out when they do. We need to do that for ourselves. Why? Because it is the right thing to do. We need first to learn how to do that, and then to teach our students how.

By waking up every morning and committing to excellence, we fulfill our destiny as teachers. We are teaching by demonstration, by knowledge and by example — and we know that the message we send is good. So here is the plan:

Commit to excellence on a daily basis.

Be true to our values.

And, above all: recognize that excellence *is* within our reach.

Master Teacher Tips

Every good teacher has come up with strategies for handling the everyday challenges of teaching. Here are a few fundamentals that bear repeating, no matter the context.

First of all, always play it straight with students. And no matter what the circumstances, never oversimplify or distort the truth to make your point. Remember, lying to authorities, including teachers, is known to flourish when students believe that those in authority are acting in bad faith. Keep in mind that if students think that the system is unfair, they may also believe that they have the right to take matters into their own hands. Needless to say, this is when discipline problems can flourish.

A technique that is very effective in changing the behavior of some student is the *reward yourself* strategy. Very seriously, (and in a private setting) say, "You need to take better care of yourself and your reputation. You need to make some people know you are capable. You need to start rewarding yourself by being the kind of person you can be." Next time you have a student, such as the late arriver or class clown, whose misbehavior is damaging his or her reputation, try this technique.

There are some quick ways to discover if you need to upgrade your discipline skills. For instance, if you have to pull rank continuously to get kids to behave, you're probably in trouble. It's a weak strategy, whether used to get students to work or behave appropriately. And an overbearing stance will lose any leverage it has in a short period of time. Rather than *using power*, try giving student incentives to behave appropriately by *sharing power*. These incentives include recognition of effort, more responsibility, study choices, more freedom, and more trust. Remember, pulling rank doesn't work over the long term. Incentives are more powerful than intimidation.

Quick action and class arrangement are two valuable tools. It's not the huge misbehaviors that steal teaching time everyday. Rather, it's low intensity, high frequency misbehaviors, such as students' talking and being out of their chairs that cause our distraction and stress. To cut both the number and frequency of these misbehaviors, we must anticipate, then we must respond calmly, firmly, and swiftly — so that the inappropriate behavior doesn't get encouraged by other students. Above all: consistent, quick, and gentle action is the key. By intervening quickly, we can better manage these misbehaviors without making mountains out of molehills. Try it, it works.

Finally, here are some important tips I've gleaned from the great teachers I've known, that sum up the essentials of good teaching:

1. Expect a lot from students based on their own ability

Don't let preconceived biases such as ethnic, racial, or social stratification interfere with your assessment. Students tend to work to their teacher's expectations. Students who receive teacher encouragement perform well. Students who sense that a teacher doesn't expect much tend to perform poorly. Demand the best the individual is capable of, and reward appropriately. Create excitement. If they're excited to come to class, their attendance will improve and their attention will improve. Remember: student achievement is 15% aptitude, 85% attitude.

2. What you give to students, fellow teachers, administration, friends, and family is what you get in return.

Smile; sell yourself and your subject. Give compliments; avoid insults. Focus on a student's strengths.

3. Don't confuse knowing your subject with being a good teacher.

Some teachers think that the more they know about their subject, the better they can teach. By all means, learn as much information as you can, but never equate the quality of teaching with the amount of knowledge you possess.

The best teachers are the ones who are constantly teaching *values*, such as self-worth, the importance of marketable skills, and a positive attitude. Students will respond to your ability to relate to them.

4. Never publicly shame for poor performance — it breaks character.

Teachers want to build character. Shame is destructive — compliments are constructive.

5. Commit to teaching values — the Golden Rule!

Many students don't know the golden rule. Emphasize manners, respect, and common courtesy. Show respect, get respect. Sometimes the recognition takes years, but your students will remember you for it.

6. Listen to students.

Are you asking the right questions? Are you hearing the answers? Be receptive to what your students are trying to tell you. Try to see yourself through their eyes.

In Conclusion

Some people are uncomfortable with my background, in that I never finished school and I spent a lot of time "hanging out." My personal history is my own doing; I came from a wonderful family that had good values, but I simply negated their influence because I didn't want to listen. Les Correia, one of America's great academicians and Assistant Principal at Hartford High, said to me years ago, "Mark, don't you get it? You're not supposed to be doing what you're doing. You're supposed to be in jail, or out committing some crime, and here you are sharing with kids and helping people to avoid making those kinds of mistakes." Well, perhaps it's because of that very background that I'm able to do that. I hope so. One thing I'm sure of is that many Teacher's Teachers helped me, even as an adult, to find my way and to keep pursuing self improvement.

In any case, the point is that *no* situation is hopeless. Given the right motivation — and we as educators are wonderfully able to provide it — any student can become a success story and can go on to help others become one. Of course, the young Mark Mainellas stand out in the crowd because they present special problems, just as the most academically gifted students stand out because of their special accomplishments. Just don't forget about the ones in the middle who may need you the most. Look at all students as special, and you'll find that they are indeed!

When I work with students, just as when I'm in the private sector, I'm not there as a "resource" guy with answers: I'm there as a human being to share reality. Most of what I share are strategies and lessons that I myself have learned from great teachers. This is wisdom that I have learned from you, and that you have learned from one another. You who are reading this book right now are the ones who've supported me the most, and I will never forget that. Please count me among your legacy, and this book as my thank-you letter. If I have been able to help you in return, this will go a small distance toward beginning to repay all you have given me, both personally and through your students.

I hope that you will also always remember to ask yourselves the questions you have taught me to ask. Are we listening? Are we enthusiastic? Do we care? Are we making eye contact with our students? Are we showing our students respect? Are we connecting with each and every one of them? Post these questions on your mirror so that you see them every morning. They are questions that can never be asked too often. It is most important that the student knows that you care about them.

Remember also that you have boundaries, and teach your students to find theirs. No teacher, no family member, no friend has the right to tell others what they can't do, to put them down, or to make them feel bad. Do your students know that? Personally, I believe that most of them do. But you must help them reinforce it by showing them that you know it also, and that it really is the truth. That will go a long way toward giving them the confidence and the self-respect they need to succeed.

So, in sum, here is our plan:

It's a plan for committing to excellence. Find what it is that you truly love doing, and then focus on being the best that you can be.

It's a plan for getting the most from your students. Get the most by *giving* them the most. Show them respect, and show them self-respect by example. This simple system of values is a lesson worth a lifetime, and they will return it — to you, to themselves and to the future — a thousand fold.

It's a plan for losing the fear and becoming the teacher's teacher. If you've come this far, then you're well on your way! Continually review these principles and keep them always within your sight. Most of all, though, be proud of yourself. You have earned it.

Chapter 11

People That Made a Difference

The final chapter is a reflection of everything that has been put down; including some inspirational characters, people who have inspired me, people who have affected my attitude in regard to who I am. Coming from an environment where many people put *things* above all else, material goods as being the ultimate goal in one's life; to have the biggest house, the fastest car, the biggest boat, the most expensive clothes, jewelry, etc; I have found peace in my life by realizing that happiness is not about accumulating things, its about the quality of the relationships.

I had to rethink my own value system. By the time I was 12 years old, my core values were established; being true to oneself, being the best that you can be, putting family first and foremost, and that friends don't laugh at their friends they laugh with their friends. I was always told that you become like who you associate with, and I chose to associate with some people whose values were completely opposite of mine. It took years of introspective thought to reevaluate, reassess, and to understand that was not the way I wanted to live. The truth is I did many things, for which I am sorry. But I did learn, and I have moved on. Objective self-assessment is always difficult, but it pays great dividends. I am at a point in my life now, where I would rather be *alone* than to spend time with people who I thought were my friends, who I thought cared about me, who actually made me feel bad about who I am.

From the time, I was 19 years old; I was married and had a new goal in life, which was to do as much good, to create as much happiness, and to be the best I could be. I stumbled along the way and I caused grief for my family and myself because on occasion I would go against my own core values. It is one thing if you have no values, a sociopath can do anything, and there is no remorse because there are no feelings. It is when you go against your own values, whatever they may be, that you create an internal schism. I am far from being as good a person as the words I share everyday, but my goal is always to be a better human being and to help others to be better human beings based on my life experience.

This chapter is an afterthought. It is October 2008 and the book was completed four years ago, but I knew something was missing. I want to put on these pages, the names of individuals, and how they have affected my life. Without the grace of God and the support of my family, and the great teachers who have continually inspired me, I would not be where I am today.

Personally, there are many great influences, role models I had, that I did not appreciate until later in life. First were my father and mother. My father was a man of tremendous principle, a sensitive kind man. He could be brought to tears by people who were not as fortunate as he was; people who had needs, and for whatever reason could not help themselves. I was a kid in the early 1950s and he was in tears watching a special about kids in third world nations. I did not understand it then, but he had a tremendous heart. He respected everyone, no matter what their status. I never heard him make disparaging remarks about any group of people (whether it be race, religion, etc). His personal creed was to find something you love doing, be the best that you can be. If you love your work and perform it well, work seeks you out. And in the truest sense of the word *work*, you'll never work a day in your life. ***And he never did.***

As far as my mother, she just said "always tell the truth, be the best you can be." Her love for her family, her passion for cooking, her desire to make everything right for everyone, continues to inspire me. My two sisters Marie and Gloria were like mothers to me. What else can I say? They were sisters, mothers, and friends.

I had a difficult relationship with my brother. We were ten years apart, and as a young man, I lived in his shadow. He was a world-class sailor and a virtuoso piano player. He knew many of the greats of rock n roll. He introduced me to a lot of old blues people, and I admired him greatly. Unfortunately as he got older, he lost sight of the value of relationships, and he focused on the accumulation of things, acquiring material goods, and that created a problem for us. However, he was a great guy and inspired me in many ways. I learned many of life's lessons from him, good and bad.

My wife is my strongest supporter; she is my most severe critic. She has always told me what I needed to hear not what I wanted to hear. Unfortunately, I have done some things that have hurt her, hurt our family and me drastically. Only through the grace of god and the strength of our love, in addition to my learning to respect her and our family, we have put things back together and have a better relationship today than ever before. They say you look in someone's eyes to read their character, the eyes are the porthole to the soul, I knew her in seventh grade, aside from being attractive on the outside, she was attractive on the inside. She was as nice a person as I had ever met.

Years later when we started to date in 1965, we used to have great philosophical discussions about the nature of man. Socrates was and continues to be philosophically a role model for me.

She always believed that people were basically good, and at that point, in my life I had the mindset that people were basically bad, and that they only did good through fear of punishment. She has been a guiding force, is the love of my life, and has always been my anchor. I cannot say enough about her intelligence, wisdom, and strength of character.

My daughter Katy, has inspired me throughout her life. She has been through some very difficult times with personal issues, revolving around self-image. I have fought with many of those issues myself. Besides being beautiful on the outside, she is beautiful on the inside, and has taught me never to compare myself, and never to accept comparison. Her husband Doug, has great strength of character; he is a father, husband and just a great person. They have two gorgeous children. I had never understood when people would describe the love for their grandchildren. It is not a better relationship, than with your own children, but a different relationship. We are crazy about little Julia and Grace, Katy and Doug's children, and little Louis and Vincent, our son Mark and Kristina's children.

My son Mark is a surgeon. Someone recently said to me, "You must be proud of your son for being a surgeon." I am proud of my son, not because he is a surgeon, but because of his character. He has the same respect for those who work with their hands, who are committed to excellence, as he has for a world-class surgeon who has good values. He married a woman who reflects those same values, she happens to be a veterinarian, Kristina, and they brought two marvelous children into this world, little Louis and Vincent.

My son contracted a form of cancer and I was crying like a baby asking "why?" His answer was "why does anyone get cancer?" I was out of control, and he said, "Dad, help me beat this thing, or leave me alone. I can't have you acting like a baby in my time of need." I celebrate each day due to the fact that Mark is 100% cancer free and healthy. If he were not a surgeon, and he were building car engines as my dad did, with his character and passion, I would be as proud. I was offended recently when someone said that it was a good thing that he did not go into the automobile business, suggesting that my son was above that. However, he was not, and he says to me that someday he might pursue that as a vocation.

My brother-in-law Joe Pezzullo, was a father, a brother-in-law, and a friend. I worked for him. He was a superintendent and project manager for Gilbane Construction. He worked his way up from a laborer. He never had the opportunity to go to college, but his success was unequalled in the construction industry. Besides possessing engineering genius, he was the essence of "lets get it done on time and on budget." Joe was in a league of his own. He was a decorated Korean veteran, and he had a profound effect on my life. Always do the best you can do, never compare yourself, and never accept comparison. He had obviously had to deal with that type of thing because he did not have the degree. He demonstrated his capabilities by producing. He was one of Gilbane's top superintendents and project managers.

We keep coming back to the quality of our lives is directly related to the quality of the relationships we have. Maybe worse today than ever before, the kids call it *the bling.* I call it the glitter and the glitz. Everyone wants things; they want the bling. However, having been there, and having come close to losing everything a number of times, I believe with certainty that true happiness is about having quality relationships. Whether it is through marriage, family, friendship, or those we work with, it is our relationships that give our lives value.

At 60 plus years old now, its more profound than ever, being able to reflect back and see people who had great wealth. For example, Elvis Presley, who I loved, and so many others in the entertainment industry. They lived such jaded lives because the pursuit of things, fame and fortune, got in the way of the relationships that they had. They had people around them who only wanted to be with them for the things that they could provide. They had the bling, but had no one to tell them to stay grounded, and to think of how their words and actions are not just affecting themselves but others.

In this last chapter, I want to reflect on some individuals and relationships besides family that have made me a stronger, better and hopefully a wiser person. This is an incomplete list of people who I have worked with over the last 35 years. Unfortunately some have passed on; many others have retired.

Friends

I guess we start with Paul Baggott. Paul is a character that I have known since kindergarten. He is a great guy, we went our different ways intermittently and we always came back. He did not get married until he was in his forties. I was married in my teens. He has a daughter today, who is sixteen years old that we just love to death. She is very close to my granddaughter, Julia. Paul and his wife Carol, are people that through circumstances could be elitist snobs. They have the opportunity to possess anything they want in terms of material goods and all they do is help others who are not as fortunate. I have had arguments with Paul on occasion in regard to why he does not buy certain things for he and his family. Paul has always related to me that things do not mean anything. It is all about relationships. I admire and respect him and his family for that reason.

I met Ed Cozzi about 20-25 years ago. He is the high performance guru down in Florida. He came from Chicago to join Howard Quam's racing team "Flapjacks". He did rigging himself and was involved in sales. For the last decade, he established himself as the premier *"go fast expert"*. He is a surveyor. He does all kinds of boats, but particularly high performance. In the most recent political campaign, there was much discussion about certain candidate's lack of experience. It forced me to think of my own life's experience, delving into projects that I knew little about. I was rebuilding an old Formula performance boat. I turned immediately to Ed because of his experience. Everything turned out beyond our expectations. The point being, we all lack experience in certain areas of our lives. That is the importance of being able to tap into the relationships that we have. To learn from those who know what we do not know. I laugh when they say that these politicians do not have experience. In any business what you need is good common sense and the means by which you can get people to help you solve the problems you may have. You need people who share your value system. When it comes to boats, cars, motors, Cozzi has more knowledge and experience than anyone I know.

Len and Carol Camuso, Wisdom personified – great character, continues to teach and inspire me. I admire them and their family immensely.

David and Kitty Stewart, David is the toughest guy I fought. Kitty is the personification of class.

Dr Giovanni & Pat Moran Mannella, Great values, great character and so many laughs together. A constant education.

Hank Coleman, A lifetime of friedship and always upbeat.

Reflecting on some people who have had an affect on my life:

Tommy Bain is a body builder in his mid 60s who looks to be in his early 40s. From when I was 10 years old, he was a role model in terms of his tenacity and willpower in regard to his diet. I still admire him to this day. He has tremendous self-control, for his physical well being, among other things. He later became friends with Steve Reeves the original Hercules of Hollywood and they trained together. He has shared with me, throughout his life, the importance of maintaining personal integrity. Tommy has great character.

Steve "Woody" Woodham, a guy who has made some mistakes in his life but has a great overall philosophy of life and a great attitude.

Vinny "Paz" is a *five- time world champion boxer*. I've known him for years. The last few years he's come out on the road with me after his career ended as a boxer. He decided he would like to share some strategies that he used to overcome a broken neck caused by an automobile accident he was in. These strategies helped him to come back and regain the title, winning another championship. Paz now travels all over the country sharing his insight in dealing with life's adversities. Paz has inspired me in so many ways, but mostly his tenacity. Paz has an extraordinary capability to deal with all sorts of physical pain, and is a tremendously inspirational guy who has inspired me. His motto is "never say die". Soon there is to be a movie on his life, so that many more will be inspired as I have been.

Recent News Paper article:

Joseph Artuso was born in the Belmont section of the Bronx to Vincent and Betty. His father started the Artuso Pastry business on 187th Street in 1946, his mother also worked in the family business. He has three brothers, Vincent, Anthony, and John.

Joe graduated from St. Martin of Tours. He started working in the family business at the age of eight.

At the age of 18 he married his childhood sweetheart, Linda Restaino, a graduate of Mt. Carmel School, with a BSW from Ramapo College. They were married at Mt. Carmel Church and have been married for 44 years. They have two children, Michele and Joseph, along with three granddaughters, Sabrina, Gabrielle, and Alexandra. Joe believes God put Linda in his life for so many wonderful reasons, especially to help him get through the rough times.

As a young man Joe became involved in the streets and paid dearly. He turned his life around and is on a mission. As he would phrase it, " from crime to Christ." He cares deeply for everyone and touches everyone he meets. He arrives each morning at his place of business, which he owns with his brother Anthony, at 3:30AM. At this time, he is not only starting the

ovens but also helping the people in the community. He takes
time out to listen and give them hope.

For the past 16 years, he has been involved with finding some
people shelter, giving food, gathering clothes, furniture, and toys
from family and friends, while directing others to the proper
resources. He always displays kindness and compassion.

Joe has been given the pleasure to see many of these people
turn their lives around too. Some came off drugs and alcohol
and others away from crime and are living productive lives. His
main goal is to show people they can change once they put
Christ in their lives.

Joe is a proud member of the Holy Name Society and has
participated in daily mass for the past 16 years.

I knew Joe's family through their bakery on 187th street in the
Bronx back in the late 1960s. Only recently we were
reacquainted. Joe is another guy who made some mistakes but
through the grace of God and a tremendous "winners attitude",
he spends his days helping others to be the best they can be. I
was complaining to him recently about finances and tough
economic times, Joe gave me the line "Mark do your best and
Jesus Christ will do the rest, so why worry." Joe and his wife
Linda, who appeared in the 1979 movie *The Wanderers,* and I
have lengthy conversations about family and values. I always
feel better after sharing with them. He just gives his heart and
soul to the world.

Dion is a very close friend of Joe and his wife Linda. Dion is
the absolute essence of 1950s and 1960s "cool". I met him in the
1960s, he was going through some very difficult times, and he
cleaned himself up and changed his entire attitude. He went out
on tour singing songs with a Christian overtone. Along with
being a world class entertainer, he teaches "the truth will set you
free".

James Brown, The first time I saw him was 1962 in New York City. Until he passed on a year ago, his commitment was to give his heart and soul to his audience. Whatever you do, do it to the best of your ability, and James did it to the best of his ability, up until the day he died.

Lynn Easton of the original Kingsmen was at the top of his game in 1963 when I met him. He had one hit after another, Louie Louie, Money, and Little Latin Lupe Lu, Valley of the Green Giant, etc. This was a guy who always mixed strong family values in with his music. He had great character.

Gary Clark, a childhood chum, always did most everything right. He was a dear friend and my lawyer and accountant. He always says to me, "it is easier to do it the right way, than to do it the wrong way and have to go back." He is a perfectionist, a stickler for everything being in order.

Mark and Palmina Arpino, In 1981, I was four or five years into lecturing in the Boston area. A small school, Newbury Junior College was sponsoring me. I was not there but maybe a week or two when I met a young lady who was finishing her Associate's Degree. She was a work-study student who, after graduation, would start working as a full-time Administrative Assistant for the Admissions Office. As I needed someone to transcribe from my dictation my "Keys to Success" lecture, she was assigned to work with me. I was told that she was one of the top students to ever attend the College. Certainly, she had the required skills. More importantly, she would be able to handle my digressions. I can be a very tough person to deal with on that level because I am moving so fast. I later found out that she was told that the results of the time we spent together were part of her pre-employment screening; when in fact, she was chosen for her ability to be able to keep up with me. We started at eight in the morning, and at about two in the afternoon, she asked me if she could take a quick break. I was aghast! We had been working feverishly in a little conference room for six straight hours! I apologized and she laughed; the rest is history. Not only did she earn my respect then, but today, twenty eight years later she, her husband and children have become like family.

Palmina came from Italy at the age of thirteen, had never spoken the English language, and was in a school system that did not embrace diversity. The point of the story with Palmina is that she has not done well, she has done extraordinarily well. As many do, she could have used every excuse (coming from a foreign country, not having great financial support, etc) but she found a way to overcome life's obstacles and pursue her dream. Palmina has been very successful in her profession as a Senior Human Resource Manager. As I write this, she is pursuing a master's degree in Management with a concentration in Organizational Development from Salve Regina University in Newport, RI. Palmina is a perfect example of one who has identified her strengths and has built a career focused on maximizing her strengths. It is all about strength of character, focus, and commitment. She and her husband have it all.

Palmina's husband Mark, who was engaged to her at the time, he and I connected 28 years ago because we share similar interests. Although Mark and Palmina are much younger than I, we share the same values, grace of God, and strength of family. His motivation is to continually pursue excellence, to be the best at whatever task that he under takes. They have continually inspired me, and now I am working with their daughter Roselle in completing this book. I have worked in their son Luke's high school, Bishop Feehan, and their daughter's school, Attleboro High School.

Mark is a person who continues to inspire me. Mark did not have the opportunity to continue his education after high school, instead he learned on the job in the electronics industry. Even in the beginning, the company recognized his work ethic and sent him to technical school at night for electronics education. He continued working full time, which only allowed him to progress much faster. He wound up at USA Broadcasting, as the

Chief Engineer of a television station, literally running the entire show. From that he went to work for a major computer corporation, and does very well. He has continued to inspire me with his commitment to whatever he does, to doing the best that he can do. Many wives would have said, "I don't want to be alone at night, we just got married," thus inhibiting their husband's potential. But the willingness of Palmina and Mark to make sacrifices only allowed them to experience greater successes.

What has carried Mark forward, and continues to carry Mark forward is his work ethic, his tenacity, and his commitment to getting the job done. Whether it means staying late, going in early, doing without lunch, or going without a coffee break, I see within him the traits that not only I personally admire, but are universal qualities among those who ultimately achieve excellence in their chosen field (*It's all about character. It's all about attitude.*). Now working with Roselle it just comes full circle. They are tremendous people who have great values, who have accomplished great things just by being the best they can be, versus using excuses to justify being less than what they can be.

The Viera brothers: Manny Viera, Master mechanic, artist, pure genius. James Viera, Ultra talented marketing and business entrepreneur should be teaching business at Stamford, Wharton, and Harvard School of Business.

There is nothing wrong with being born on third base or being born with a silver spoon. What is wrong is if you are insensitive to those who were not and thinking that you are better than other people. What is wrong is being insensitive to the diversity in our world. *There is nothing wrong with having things, because we all want things. What we need to focus on is the fact that life's greatest pleasures come when we give to others what we want for ourselves; love, respect and friendship. Creating quality relationships.*

Appendix I Recommended Reading:

1. *You Can Heal Your Life* by Louis Hay
2. *Life 101* by John Roger and Peter McWilliams
3. *Your Erroneous Zones* by Dr. Wayne W. Dyer
4. *Healing the Shame that Blinds You* by John Bradshaw
5. *Bradshaw — On the Family* by John Bradshaw
6. *Notes to Myself* by Hugh Prather
7. *The Power of Positive Thinking* by Dr. Norman Vincent Peale
8. *Chicken Soup for the Soul* by Jack Canfield and Mark Victor Hansen
9. *Greater Expectations, Overcoming the Culture of Indulgence in America's Homes and Schools* by William Damon
10. Everything by Leo Buscaglia
11. Everything by Tony Robbins
12. Everything by Zig Ziglar
13. *When the bough breaks: the cost of neglecting our children* by Sylvia Ann Hewlett
14. *The Prophet*
15. *Head first* by Norman Cousins
16. *All I Really Need to Know I Learned in Kindergarten* by Robert Fulghum
17. *The Seven Habits of High Effective People* by Steven R. Covey
18. *The Power of Focus* by Jack Canfield, Mark Victor Hansen, and Les Hewitt
19. *Teacher Man & Angela's Ashes* by Frank McCourt
20. *Mentors, Masters, and Mrs. McGregor* Compiled by Jaden Lewenstein, PHD
21. *Higher Education in American Society* by Philip G. Autbach and Robert O. Burdahl
22. *Moments For Teachers* by Robert Strand
23. *My Way* by Frank N. Mickens
24. *Learning to be Literacy Teachers in Urban Schools* by Althier M. Lazar

25. *Pygmalion in the Classroom* by Robert Rosentral, PHD, and Lenor Jacobson EdPHD
26. *Who Moved my Cheese* by Spencer Johnson, MD
27. *Creating a Learning Environment* by John M. Brucato
28. *The Faculty Parking Lot is not for Planning* James L. Conro
29. *Reflections of an Urban High School Principal* Bernard Gassaway
30. *Everything by* Dr. Theodore Sizer
31. *Forty-Eight Days To The Work You Love* by Dan Miller
32. *The Schools Our Children Deserve* by Alfie Khon

Appendix II   Recommended Movies:

I want to list some "must see movies" for kids, for teachers, for parents. If you have connected with anything I have written here, then I guarantee that these movies will touch you on some level. So why do we look at movies, because they inspire us. Just because things are not necessarily the way they should be does not mean that we should not strive to make things better.

1. All of Frank Capra's films- *It's a Wonderful Life, Mr. Smith Goes to Washington, Mr. Deeds Comes to Town, Meet John Doe* - all of his films inspire me, its good over evil, its right over wrong. It's the way it should be, whether it is that way in reality or not, it is the way it should be in these films.
2. *Miracle on 34th Street* (Original Version)-
3. *A Christmas Carol*—1951 Alistair Simms Version
4. *Rudy-* Was told he was not college material, went to community college, then transferred to Notre Dame and graduated top of his class.
5. *Heidi*—Shirley Temple
6. *Iron Will*
7. *My Left Foot-* Overcoming life's obstacles
8. *Knute Rockne All American*
9. *Stand and Deliver*
10. *The Hustler* (Paul Newman & Jackie Gleason)

11. *Greatest Game Ever Played*
12. *Breaking Away*
13. *Hoosiers*
14. *Mr. Holland's Opus*
15. *Blackboard Jungle*
16. *American Me* (The central issue is self respect)
17. Johnny Depp Movies: *Benny and June* and *What's eating Gilbert Grape?*
18. *Lean on Me*
19. *Good Will Hunting*
20. *Shindler's List*
21. *Radio* with Cuba Gooding
22. *Elephant Man*
23. *Hunchback of Notre Dame* (With Mareen O'Hara and Charles Laughton)
24. *Casablanca* (almost everything Bogie did)
25. *Somebody up there likes me* (True Life story of Rocky Graziano starring Paul Newman)
26. *Rocky* (Only the first one)
27. *The Natural* (With Robert Redford)
28. *Brian Picalo Story* (staring James Cann)
29. *The Bucket List* (With Morgan Freeman and Jack Nicholson)
30. *Gandhi (Staring Ben Kingsley)*
31. *Field of Dreams*
32. *Shaw shank redemption*
33. *Coal Miner's Daughter*
34. *Braveheart*
35. *Life is Beautiful*
36. *Dead Poet's Society*
37. *Slum Dog Millionaire*

Appendix III   Acknowledgements:

I would like to acknowledge some ongoing relationships, some of which have been for nearly sixty years. Friends never betray their friends. Friends never laugh at their friends, they always laugh with their friends.

The Hanscoms, Jane, Lanny and family. Just beautiful people with great values.

The Quigleys. Paul and Geneva. Their children and their grandchildren. World class golfers, world class characters.

Steven Prout, known as "Panama" by many, but few know Steve as well as I. Since 1953, we have shared so many of life's experiences, and I am a stronger person for having him as a loyal supportive friend.

Adelino Almeida and his family. We were involved in a restoration project approximately 15 years ago, and we were given his name by a mutual friend Nelson Hawkins, an old timer in the marine industry. He said that if you wanted the best, whether it be wood, fiberglass, or whatever, get Adelino. We did get him, and his skills proved to be superior, but most importantly, his character, his honesty, his attitude have allowed us to become great friends.

Joe Balasco Always giving, always striving to present the highest quality products to his customers.

Lets now make mention of just some of the great academicians that have allowed me to stand on their shoulders and share the truth.

<u>Rhode Island</u>

Dr. Arthur Zarrella, principal of Classical High School, later superintendent of Providence Schools, opened so many doors for me because of the respect his peers had for him, putting kids first.

Paul Guneris, principal of Hope High School, totally committed to a very difficult population.

Steve Peppin director of guidance at Warren High School. I now work with his son in the guidance office of North Smithfield High School. What connects them besides their blood is that they put students first.

Paul Rotchford, principal of Middletown High School, helped me get into Roger Williams University after I got my G.E.D.

Ed Miley, principal of Warwick Vets, the first school I ever lectured in. He said, "Make a difference, offer some value, or I'll personally throw you out of my school."

Dr. Vic Mercurio, principal of Pilgrim, now superintendent of East Greenwich schools. I lectured to Vic's senior class when he was a student at Bishop Hendricken.

Ira Brown at Woonsocket High School, Tollman High School, Mashpee High School, Springfield High School of Science and Technology. When we first met he shared with me that after listening to my lecture for a couple of minutes he wanted to have me removed from his building, he then stated that as he further listened he realized that his and my values were one and the same, helping kids to live their dreams.

Arthur Almasion at East Providence High School. I saw students seek him out just to get a smile and a compliment.

Joseph Adamec at Bishop Hendicken High School. Joe says every year when he introduces me to his students, "Mark you're going to speak to the best and the brightest."

Dr. Stanley Thompson, had me work in West Bay Voc, Coventry High School, Rogers High School and Times 2rd Academy. Now director of the Hines Foundation in Pittsburg, always talked about values, character building, and putting students first.

Sue Tessier, Mount Saint Charles Academy. Sue always told me that her students are the best and the brightest.

Joe Goho, who said, "we are about building character at North Providence High School along with the pursuit of academic excellence."

Kevin Sheehan, Pilgrim High School, North Smithfield High School, South Kingston High School, Johnston High School. Kevin said, "I want you to offer value, not only to our best and brightest, but to those who need it the most."

Gerry Habershaw, Principal of Warwick Vets High School, Gerry cares so much about his students he says " I would never leave, we have the best teachers, the best kids". And Gerry goes so far as to get me booked at Warwick Area Tech Facility and makes the extraordinary effort to introduce me to director and students.

Connecticut

Dr. Goldstone in Warren G. Harding High School and Amity High School. Could have worked anywhere, but chose a school where he felt he could make the most difference.

Tom Duffy at Bristol Central High School and Enfield High School. Tom's a Philadelphia native who has helped me to be a better speaker in more ways than I can count.

James L. Conro, author of *The Faculty Parking Lot is Not For Planning* from Coventry High School, Palmer High School, Wachona High School. I have worked with Jim over two dozen times. His expectations are of the highest order. I have never had less than a super session.

Everett Walens at Danbury High School. Everett introduced me to approximately 1,000 ninth graders and then to approximately 600 seniors. You could hear a pin drop for the three hours I was with both classes. The respect he gave his students, they in turn gave me, out of respect for him.

Dr. Petrozillo at Greenwich High School. I once commented to her that even if I were blindfolded when entering the school grounds I would know that I was at Greenwich if I were allowed to touch the hood ornaments in the faculty parking lot. She said to me, "Mark you've got it all wrong those aren't our teachers' automobiles, those are our students' automobiles".

Dr. Frizzell at Griswold High School. A Marine, a Principal, a family man, and a human being who passionately cares about kids.

Dr. Brian K. Mignault, Sr H.H. Ellis Technical High School Danielson, CT "No excuses, be the best that you can be."

Diane McNicholas-Butsockis at H.C. Wilcox Regional High School. Not enough accolades to describe her commitment to kids.

Les Coria, Hartford Public High School. Grew up in Spanish Harlem, and spent his life giving back to the kids that needed him the most. He taught me so much, especially when we would share time in New York City back on the streets.

Dr. John J. Ramos, Alternative Learning Project, Norwolk High School, Watertown High School, Bridgeport High School. For over 25 years, Doc has demonstrated to me, his commitment to putting students first.

Scott Schoonmacher, Superintendent of North Branford school. Scott represents the new blood that embraces the old values that state, along with academic excellence we must focus on building strength of character. No one has been more supportive of my efforts than Scott. I recently saw a life changing event at his school, when he invited me in to listen to the anti-defamation league conduct a sensitivity session for students at Old Say Brook. The entire population, ninth through twelfth grade was given the opportunity to express their feelings relevant to a typical day as a high school student. The intimate experiences that were shared by scores of students were profound. That day I saw a school embrace the values of helping one another to feel good about themselves whatever shape, size, background, color etc. It should happen in every school.

Henney Budnick, Wolcott High School. Always making a difference.

Bruce Seivers, Steve Anderson, Art Arpin, They all say "I love the kids, I love what I do, I love making a difference".

Massachusetts

Dr. Manville, Beverly High School and Saugus High School. Always told me "let them know you care. They will respond".

Cornelia Kelley, Boston Latin High School. "Our students aren't better, they are different," she used to say, "they are academically elite, but they still have baggage. It's often of a different sort. Help them to be the best that they can be".

Mike Donato, Hyde Park High School. Mike was instrumental in my success in Boston schools.

Les Murray, Amesbury High School, Timberlane High School. No one cares more about students than Les.

Phil Charbineau, Bartlett High School, one of the first to have me with eighth graders as well as his high school students.

Roland Joyal, Chicapee High School. Roland comes from a family with a history of academic leadership. Another of the new blood that cares passionately about helping his students to be the best that they can be.

Bret Kustigian, formerly Douglass High School principal. He was a student at one of my lectures and is currently the Superintendent for the Quaboag Regional School District.

Dr. William Goodwin, Gloucester High School. He said, "Mark we are all about building character at Gloucester."

Brian Bentley, Diman Regional Voc. Tech. Always tells me "Diman is second to none."

Dave Driscoll, Whether in Massachusetts or Vermont, whether with students or staff, Dave always set me up for a win.

John Brucato, author of *Creating A Learning Environment,* always talked to me about creating a culture of mutual respect.

Bob and Linda Gay, North Attleboro High School, Whitman Hanson High School. What can I say, the best of the best.

Mark Condon, Pathfinder Regional Vocational Technical. With his students, with his staff, it's always the same. Excellent.

Richard (Dick) Najarian, Watertown High School. Dick always told me, "Student's first."

Don Pelligrini, West Roxbury High School. Don had a profound affect on my career. He was the youngest principal ever in the city of Boston. I started with him in 1978, and although he is now retired as a principal, he has ended up in Providence mentoring administrators in their schools. They say that the best are attracted to the best. Whether that's true or not, Don has always been to me, the best of the best.

Appendix IV   MSSAA Friend of Education Award:

Article from Massachusetts Secondary School Administrators Association, Inc "MSSAA Leader" publication:

Noted Inspirational Speaker Mark Mainella is Named "Friend of Education" By MSSAA

*President Bob Gay Congratulates Mark Mainella
following the award presentation*

At the enthusiastic recommendation of many of our members, MSSAA is pleased to recognize the work of Mark Mainella, who has been an inspiration speaker in many of our schools for over 20 years. His message combine a powerful appeal to what is best in our students with personal dynamism that captures the attention and enthusiasm of his audience.

One of our members states that, "for the past 26 years, Mark Mainella remains one of the best speakers to visit our school. His message conveys a sense of reality in regard to the unlimited human potential. He is appreciated and we greatly value his efforts to help our students and staff reach their maximum potential. We would never go a year without his presentation. "

In making the presentation, MSSA President Bob Gay noted that he and his family had become personal friends of Mark Mainella over the years, and expressed his own admiration for the manner in which Mark caught and held the attention and respect of the students to whom he spoke. He noted that the effect upon students who heard Mr Mainella was palable and that his message was always on point and delivered in a way that maximized its impact on the thinking of those in his audience.

In a period when students are subjected to so many questionable messages and many distractions, MSSAA takes a very appropriate action in recognizing Mark Mainella, always the bearer of a positive message, as a friend of all of the students he affects and naming him our "Friend of Education" for this year. We wish him well as he goes forward with his work

Appendix V   Schools where I have presented:

Connecticut

Albert Prince VT HS	Silas Shannon Jr., Bruce Sievers, Hank Weiner
Amity HS	Dr. Goldstone
Bentley Alternative School	Diane Kearney
Berlin HS	Dr. Silva, Brian Sullivan, Dr Mark Banigni, Mr Synott
Branford HS	David Maloney
Bristol-Central HS	Dr. Mike Ferry, Tom Duffy, Paul Castalleen
Bullard-Haven VT HS	Jean Marcone, Dr. Aviva Coen
Cheshire HS	Ms. Maureen Berescik
Coginchoag HS	Lynne Williams, Nancy Ryan, Nancy Leddy, Beth Galagen
Coventry HS	Will Ducheneau, Peter Francis, Gary Baumgarder, Troy Hopkins
Cromwell HS	Dr Mark Banigni
Danbury HS	John A. Goetz, Everett Walens
Daniel Hand HS	Gary Meunier
E.C. Goodwin RVT HS	John Tarnuzzer, Bill Sarmuck, Gil Taverson
East Hartford HS	Dr. Steven Edwards, Craig Jordan
East Haven HS	Steve Anderson
East Lyme HS	Tim Evers
East Windsor HS	Robert Johnson
Edwin O. Smith HS	Mark Winsler, Dr. Barbara Panarvik
Ella Grasso Vocational HS	William Enters, Mr. White
Emmett O'Brien RT HS	Lisa Hylach, Jim Frank
Enfield HS	Tom Duffy, Steven Sargalski
Greenwich HS	Dr. Petrozillo
Griswold HS	Dr. Frizzell

Guilford HS	Libby Houlihan
H.C. Wilcox Regional HS	Diane McNicholas, Mr. Cavalaro, Andy Taddie
H.H. Ellis RVT HS	Jody Heidelgerber, John Haskell, Gail Welburn, Kathy Burr, Mr. Congdon, Mr. Vega, Dr. Brian McNault, Mr Erol Groff, Mr Roland Belan, Larry Lebuff, Pat McCagen
Hamden HS	Dr. Pitkoff
Harding HS	Dr. Goldstone, Joe Debelis
Hartford Public School (2nd oldest HS in America)	Les Corria, Manny Santiago, Nilda Espada
Henry Abbott Tech HS	Mario DeLaurenzo, Geroge Quigley, Linda Swanson, Dr. Santagarda
Howell Cheeney RVT HS	Dr. Randall, Kathy Burr, Bruce Sievers,
J.M. Wright Tech HS	Dan Kushman, Andy Taddie
Killingly HS	Dave Sweet, Mr. Dodge, Mrs. Sampson, Mr. Erardi, Mary Christian
Meridian School District	Dr. Mark Banigni
Middletown HS	Hank Korticoski
Montville HS	Mike Pennalla
New Britian HS	Dan Bugnacki, Paul Salina, Dr. Reale, Dennnis Marinello, Dr. Pitkoff
North Branford HS	Dr. Perry, Todd Steffler
New London HS	Reggie Grover
Norwalk HS	Dr. John J. Ramos, Jackie Helen, Dewy Amos, Don Faust
Norwich Free Academy	Ms. Flumb
Norwich RVT HS	Charles Salerno, Eileen Ryan, Judy Leonard, Dr. Murphy,
Old Saybrook HS	Mr. Sparaco, Scott Schoonmacher, Gretchen Bushnell
Orville H. Platt HS	Timothy J. Gaffney, Joe Paluszewski, Donna Mik
Plainfield HS	Charles Langevin, Mr. Law, Mr. Dimmuck

Plainville HS	Rose-Marie Cipriano
Platt Regional Vocational HS	Vincent Casanova, Susan Rosner, Linda Evanko
Putnam HS	Nelson G. King, Mark Laurito, Dick Jacquish, Linda Joyal, Paul Brenton
Rham HS	Mary Bartolla, Carol Fish, Brendan McCarthy, Lynn Karauous
Robert E. Fitch Senior HS	Ed Bartolini, Julie Jones, John Luciano, Bob Basawitz, Mike Emory
Rockville HS	Keith Garet, Brian Levesque
Stafford	Ms Italia, Dr David Perry
Stonington HS	Dick Risio, Tom Jones, Linda DiSimone, Dr. Murphy, Jen McCurdy, Allyson Venetten
Strong Middle School	Carol DiBernado,
The Rectory School	Craig Evans
Tourtellotte Memorial HS	Art Greenside, Dr. Grenier, Dave Hackenson, Steve Mitchell
Trumbul HS	Bill Kovachi
Vinal RVT HS	Tom Scharrett, Bernie English, Henny Budnick, Linda Coolick, Spence Clapp
Waterbury HS	Mr. Lombardi
Waterford HS	Dr. Granier, Gil Amaral, Wayne Lawrence, C. Piskura, Don Macrino
Watertown HS	Fayne Malloy
WF Kaynor RTS	Lisa Hylwa
Wheeler HS	Bob Plante
Windam HS	Gene Blain
Windom RTHS	Pat Ciscone, Mitch Pietras
Wolcot HS	Henny Budnick
Wolcot RT HS	Dan Kushman
Womoko HS	John Oko
Woodstock Free Academy	Marshall Tourtellotte

Woodstock Middle School	Dave Gamache

Massachusetts

Another Course To College	
Athol HS	Kent Strong, Tom Pollito, Brian Beck
Attleboro HS	Jimmy Shine,
Auburn Senior HS	Jeffrey Theodoss, Jeff Zangi
Ayer HS	Don Parker
Bellingham HS	Mr Polito
Beverly HS	Dr. Manville, Anthony Witwicki
Boston Latin	Joseph Walsh, Cornelia Kelley, Gordon Esterbroook
Boston Latin Academy	Joe Walsh,
Charlestown HS	Mary Ann and Larry Matthews, Mr. Rafferty, Mr. Mike Donato, Kelly Flynn
East Boston HS	John Poto, Jane O'Leary, Miss Halcopulous, Gay Rafferty
Jeremiah E Burke HS	Ms. Mezzolla, Mr. Cardoza
Snowden Int'l HS	Ms Howard
Washington Irving Middle	Dr. Watson
Wm B Rogers Middle	Dr. McCarthy and Paula Pelligrini
Abington HS	Jeff Kent
Amesbury HS	Leslie Murray, Roy Hamond, Elizabeth McAndrews
Apponequet Regional HS	Peter Abraham
Arlington HS	Mr Butters
Athol HS	Charles Russel Jr, Kent Strong, Tony Polito
Attleboro HS	Pat Knox, Richard Reynolds,
Barlett HS	Mike Hackenson, Phil Charbineau
Bay Path VT	Ben Monfredo, and Kevin Wells
Billerica Memorial HS	Richard Safier, Mrs. McCarthy
Bishop Connolly	Jim McNamee

Bishop Feehan	Chris Servant, George Milot,
Bishop Stang	Jim McNamee
Blackstone Valley RVT HS	Joan McGully,
Blackstone Millville RHS	Robert Powers, Stephen Schrebitz, Rick Porter, Keith Ducharme, Kevin Maloney
Blue Hills RVT HS	Mr Smith
Boston HS	Tom Henessey, Jim Keenan, Bud Fox, Joe Clark
Bourne HS	John Grondin, John McGough, Jack Cofflin
Braintree HS	Bill Wassel
Bridgewater-Raynham	Mr. and Mrs. Casabian, Mr. Jackson, Mr. de Castro, Ms. Childs, John Lennon
Bristol County Agricultural	Russell James, Mike Shaffer, Steve Dempsey, Mark Dufresne, Missy Duffy, Miss Paynton
Bristol-Plymouth RVT HS	Jean Whelan, Tim Duffy, Steve MacAntos, Naomi Davis
Brockton HS	Ron Coccuzzo
Brooke Farm HS	Ed Donley, Rich and Bill Webber
Canton HS	
Cape Cod RVT HS	Jan Tikazik, Larry Learner, Pat Tatora, Richard Curcio, Ed McDonald, William Terranova
Carver HS	Rocky Palladino
Catholic Memorial HS	Tony Polito
Chatham HS	Mr Troy
Chelsea HS	Peter Steritie, Stu Feinburg
Chicopee HS	Roland Joyal
Chicopee Comp	Chris Theriault, Derek Morrison
Clinton Senior HS	Howard Lore
Comm ACAD of Science and Health	
Madison Park HS	Mr Watson

The English HS	Mr Bagley
Cohasset Middle/HS	Mr Riley
Dartmouth HS	Donald King, Jerry Hicky
David Prouty HS	Vito Filipkowski, Richard Gaudett, Kevin O'Leary, Kevin Wells, Dave Bachant, Rob O'Brien
Dedham HS	Paul Quatrramoni, Ken Toomy, Mr Buliwell, Alan Winrow, Jake Santarita
Dennis-Yarmouth Reg HS	Bill White,
Dighton-Rehoboth RHS	Jeff Day, Dave Marsden, Paul Lupia
Dougherty HS	Sam McCore
Dom Savio HS	Jim Dougherty
Don Basco HS	Mr. Sheets and Mr. Goff
Douglas HS	Brett Kastigian
Dover-Sherborn Reg HS	Mr. Marlboro
B.M.C. Durfee HS	Ed Morgan, Mr. Kelly and Mr. Kiely
East Bridgewater HS	Dr. Judy Reordon, Geroge Kelly, Helen Cox
Essex County Tech	Peter Dolan
Everett HS	Bob Tringali, John Miranda
Fairhaven HS	Dr. Newburn, John Haaland, Paul McGabe
Foxborough HS	Mr. Imonen, Sam Cashman, Jeff Theodoss
Franklin County RVT HS	Patty Bassett, Rick Martin
Gardner HS	Mr. Dubskinski
Gloucester HS	Dr. William Goodwin
Grafton Memorial Senior	Ray LeMay, Mr. Richardson, Mr. Casey, Dave Grenier

Diman Reg VT HS	George Latendre, Ms. Johnson, Ms. Iloitz, Ms. Kenny, Paul Nurgai, Mr. Tabecas, Brian Bentley, Ron Jr. and Sr. Silvia, John Miranda, Mike Olivera
Greater Lawrence RVT HS	Joe Golec
Greater Lowell RVT HS	Carol Bell, Mr. Nicolson
Greater New Bedford RVT HS	Mike Shea, Gene Cody, Jim Rule, Mr Oliver
Hanover HS	Ed Walsh
Harwich HS	Mr. Bresnahan, Glen Bryant, Mr. Dunford, Troy Hopkins
Haverhill HS	Mr Rogers
Hingham HS	Mr Grogan
Holbrook Jr Sr HS	Mr Staley
Holliston HS	George Thompson
Hopedale Jr Sr HS	Ron Santacroce, Joe Renda
Hopkinton HS	
Hull HS	Bob Corcoran
Hyde Park	Mike Donato, Jean Morrelli
John D. O'Byrant HS	Joseph Staples, Chief DiBose and Commander Dufresne
Joseph Case HS	Howie O'Hare, Gerry Furtado Mike Flanagan, James Conforti
Ipswich HS	Barry Cahill
King Philip Reg HS	Mike Lavine
Leicester HS	Milt J Teguis, Paul Sabella, Mrs. Rice, Tom Gribon, Tom Lauder, Mr. Sipos
Leominster Senior HS	Ed Walsh, Dr. McClean, Dr Hart, Steve Dubskinski, Tom Chiconne
Lowell HS	Walter Nelson, Jill McNamara. Tom Thornton
Classical HS	Bob Whitcher, Willian Mahoney, Gene Constantino, Mr. White

Lynn English HS	Tom Connoly
Lynn VT Institute	Dr. Jan Cheradona, Ralph Jameson, Dr. Coughlin, Pat Chicoya, Jim Lynn
Mansfield HS	Edward Rosa, Kathy Flaherty
Mashpee HS	John Williams, Ira Brown, Ms. St. Syr, Alan Winrow
Medford HS	Ms. Calari-Clark
Medway HS	Dave Driscoll, Joe Hanlon, Terry Campana, Richard Pearson, Frank Jackson
Nipmuc Regional HS	Paul Daigle, Steve Gressich, Joan Scribner
Milford HS	Kevin Manes, John Brucato
Millbury Jr/Sr HS	Dr. Stephen Mills, Charles Carporelli, Mr. Carmody
Milton HS	Dr. Fitzgerald, Joe Arango, Moran Costello
Montachusett RVT HS	John Derkzis, Steve Johnson, Dave Grenier, Nicholas DeSimone, Thomas Porter
Mt Greylock Reg HS	Russ Norton
Murdoch HS	Charlie Dephilipo
Narragansett Reg HS	
Nashoba Valley RVT HS	Bruce Carpenter, Joe Mullen, Fred Green, Paul Royte
North Cambridge Catholic	Bob McCarthy, Sister Ellen Powers
North Middlesex HS	Charlie Dephilipo
North Shore Tech	John Lynch
Nauset Regional HS	Jim Shine, Bob Milbier, Ed McDonald
New Bedford HS	Joe Oliver, Beverly Bizarro, Jared Rose, Mr. Nebron, Mike Longo, Donald Vasconcelles, Andy Kulac
Norfolk County Agricultural	Ron Cocuzzo, Michael Kelley, Kerry Cavallaro
North Attleboro HS	Bob and Linda Gay

School	Teachers
Northbridge HS	Edward Riley, Ron Saffer,
Norton HS	Renee Tellier
Norwood HS	
Old Colony RVT HS	Rick Mitchell, Dave Harrison, Ann Sparlette, Gary Brown, Gina Despres, Kevin Gonsalves, Karen Gamache, Nancy Francis
Old Rochester Reg HS	Mr. Corier
Oliver Ames HS	Wes Paul
Oxford HS	Dave Grenier, Ernie Boss, Kevin Wells
Palmer HS	Jim Conro
Pathfinder RVT HS	Mark Condon
Pittsfield HS	Mark Matthews, Mr. Wilson,
Taconic HS	Mr Hadley
Plymouth North HS	Mary Callahan, Mrs. Winoker
Plymouth South HS	Mrs. Winoker
Quabbin Regional HS	Bernie Audette, Joe Magga, Dr. Wassel, Carol Sousa
North Quincy HS	Mr. Chrisom SR, Peter Chrisom, Eileen Feeney, Dick Meyer, Lou Ioanelli,, Earl Metzler
Quincy HS	Lloyd Hill, Bob Kuther
Randolph HS	James Watson, Jerry Linehan, Don Sarney
Revere HS	Bill McAulduff jr, Ernie Caravastos, Mr. Blazaia, Mr. Cappadalupp, Jim Lawdon
Rockland Senior HS	Peter Traveline, Joe Weisgerber
Salem HS	Charlene Baily, Diane McCrane, David Angeroni, Matt Buchanan
Sandwich HS	Russ Norton, Bill Sangster, Dr. Silva, Cara Peterson, Bob Milbier
Saugus HS	Dr. Manville

Seekonk HS	Dr. Justis Anderson, Dr. Gizzi, Patty Connors
Sharon HS	Mike Lavine
Shepard Hill Regional HS	Al Thibideau, Charlie DePhilipo, Paul Daigle, Dave Grenier, Tim Shore, Sean M. Gilrein
Somerset HS	Donald Rebello, Len Alves, Charles Leary, Jim Sullivan, Bob Renault
South-Eastern RT HS	Jerome Burke
South Community HS	Peter Vuona, Andy Power, Mary Harrington, Donna Galloogly
Somerville HS	Mr. Mathers
South Shore RVT HS	Katie Schwabe, John Kosko
Springfield Central HS/Science-Tech	Bill Goodwin, Ira Brown
Putnam VT HS Sch	Roland Joyal
South Bridgewater Springfield Central HS	Bill Bishop
Sutton HS	Paul Daigle
Joseph Case HS	Howie O'Hare, Gerry Furtado
Taunton HS	Paul Dooley, Pat Jackman, Sue Grife
Tewksbury HS	Dr. Ferris, Patty Lahley
The Rogers Middle School	Dr. McCarthy, Paula Pelligrini
Tri County RVT HS	Peter Rickard, Jack Jones
Upper Cape Cod RVT HS	Barry Motta, S.F. Rodes, Kevin Phar
Wachona HS	Jim Conro, author of The Faculty Parking Lot is not for Planning
Walpole HS	Edward Turley
Wareham HS	Scott Palladino
Watertown HS	Dick Najarian, Dave Campbell
Wellesley Sr HS	Mr. Smith
West Boylston HS	Todd Solmonson

West Bridgewater Jr-Sr	Ms. Dave
Westfield VT HS	Steve Pipin, Karen Soares, Hilary Weisgerber, Steffan Zaparowski
Weston HS	
Westport HS	Tony Melli
West Roxbury HS	Don Pellegrini, Jack Miller, Susan Friel, Ed Donley, Rich and Bill Webber
Weymouth HS	Mr. Giorse
Whitman Hanson Regional	Bob Gay, Linda Gay, Mr. Alperin, Ed Walsh, Mr. Don Sullivan, Pam Gould
Winthrop Sr HS	Dr. Nazzaro, Bob Capezza, Steve Chrabaszcz
Woburn HS	John Carr
Burncoat Senior HS	Dr. William B. Hynes, Bill Abraham, William Folley, Dave Nolan
Worcester Technical HS	

Rhode Island

School Name	Contact Person
Babcock Middle School	Jim Gurino
Bishop Hendrickson HS	Joseph Adamec, John Jackson, George Coombs
Bristol HS	Ms. Britto
Burriville HS	Ron Brissette, Steve Mitchell
Central Falls Junior/Senior HS	Charlie VanGordon, Arthur Patenaude, Nadien Greene, Bob Patenaude, Jeff Schoneh, Bruce Macsood, Jack Lyle
Classical HS	Dr. Arthur Zarrella, Scott Barr
Cranston East HS	Don Babbott, Mr. Vendatulo
Cranston West HS	Lyle Perra
Chariho Regional HS	Edward P. Morgan, Dr. Vetelino, Mr. Toscano, Mr. Kenyon, and Dr. Dillon

Coventry HS	Dr. Stanley Thompson
Charles E. Shea Senior HS	James F. MacNaught, Mr. Lemiew, Dr. Lord
Cumberland HS	Rose Marie Cipriano, Joan LaPlant, Dick Lynch
East Greenwich HS	Mike Levine
East Providence Senior HS	Arthur Elmasian, Ed Cronin, Ed Daft, Ray Lombardo, Dr. Caswel, John Craig
Exeter-West Greenwich	Brian Butler
Hope HS	Pat Newell, Paul Guneris, Mr. Badway, Dr. Petrozillo
Johnston Senior HS	Brian Abadallah, Mr. Acchili, Ray Flanagan, Wilma Palmaccio, Mary Christian, Dr Mantili, Brian Butler, Joe Neri, Al Fredda
LaSalle Academy	Richard Larkin, Don Cavanaugh, Ed Cronin
Lincoln HS	Kevin Wells, Lem Crooks, Bob Martin, Kevin McNamara
Middletown HS	Paul Rotchford, Mr. Coen, Mr. Mello (English teacher), Dr. Lord
Mount Pleasant HS	Maria Wilks, Ralph Matera, Mr. Porter, Ed DiPrete
Mount St. Charles Academy	Susan Tessier, Steve Bartow, Brother John, Hank Ferry, Rene Tellier, Mrs. Ferry
Narragansett HS	Bill Pipin
North Providence HS	Joe Goho, Lucile DeLasanta, Mr. Flaherty
North Smithfield Middle/Senior HS	Dave Silva, Tony Liotis, Bill Pipin, Kevin Sheehan, Tom Mezzonti
Pilgrim HS	Edmund P. Miley, Tom Dolce, Victor MicCurio, Dennis Mullen, Jim Ginolfi
Ponaganset HS	Dr. Oswald, Susan Poor, Steve Mitchell
Rogers HS	Dr. Stan Thompson, Mike Lopes, Jack Harrington
Times ²rd Academy	Dr Stan Thompson, David Estes

Tiverton	Steve Chrabaszcz, Mr Cabral, Al Malgeri
Warwick Veterans Memorial HS	Ed Miley, Dave Desantis, Gerry Habersaw, Walter Guest, Larry West, Darren Cipriano
West Warwick	Mr Talbot, Mrs Soarse
Westerly	Paula Fasco, James Gurino
Warwick Area Technical Facility	Bill McCaffrey
Woonsocket	Carnel Henderson

Vermont

Bellows Free Academy	Claude Bouchard, Mr. Godin
Harwood Union HS	Dave Driscoll
Barre Regional VTC	Walter Dowling

Pennsylvania

Philadelphia HS of Motivation
and various other inner city
schools

New Jersey

Atlantic City HS
Patterson HS
Newark Various Schools

New Hampshire

Alton HS	George Rogers
Alverne HS	Ms. Foley
Concord HS	Tim Mayes
Manchester Central HS	Roland Blanchard
Manchester School of Tech	John Rist
Pinkerton Academy	William "Woody" Wood, Chuck Varney, Mr. Ek, Jack Grube

Salem HS	Marshall Dery, Dick Cardner, Debbie Martel, Austen Garafalo, Linda McCaulisk
Nashua HS	Patrick Corbin
Timberlane HS	Bill Mealy, Dr. Carter, Les Murray
Winnacunnet HS	Jude Ann Langlois
Exeter HS	Eileen Sheehey
Holice-Brookline HS	Ron Ruda

Maine

Biddeford HS	Warren G. Galway
Edward Little HS	Dr. Steve Galway
Gardner HS	Roger Lachapelle
Kennbunk HS	Mike LeVerrieur, Dr. Ferris
Lewiston HS	Roger Lachapelle, Shaun Lambert
Telstar HS	Shaun Lambert,
Wells HS	Marty Ryan

Florida

Miami Jackson HS	
Osceola HS	Norma Evans O'Connor
Poinciana HS	Cebra Pace, Charity Vickers, Leslie Dubin, Lorine Guzman
Sunrise HS	

New York

Automotive HS	Margaret Meehand, Bernadine Mignano, Dr. William Salzman
Aviation HS	Eileen Taylor, Dino Churalumbus
Beach Channel HS	Bob Coomer, Dr. Morris, Bernard Gassaway
Boys and Girls HS	
Co-op Teachnical HS	Roberta Goldberg, Mark Satine
Columbus HS	Eilieen Burke
Crotona Academy	Mr. Anthony Harris

Ellenville HS	Sherry DiSimone, Mark Ellison
Far Rockaway HS	Mark Goldberg
Franklin K. Lane HS	Paul Padota, Mary Ellen Kellen, Pehonix Hodge
George Westinghouse IT HS	Shelly Wald
Grace Dodge Career & Technical HS	Mrs. Neshi
Graphic Communications Arts HS	Anthony Harmon, Pat Delaney,
HS of Telecommunications	John Tumonaro, Barbara Mahr
John Adams HS	Rich D'Auria, Linda and Juan Martinez
Lewis D. Brandeis HS	Pat Condi, Suzanne Koczinski
Liberation Diploma Plus HS	April Leong
Matthan Leaning Center	Etel Elman
Norman Thomas HS	Miss Lang, Mr. Cohen
Park West HS	JoAnn Kestin, Brian Wallach, Phil Schrank, Jeff Kellerman
Porchester HS	Mark Santoro, Kevin Delcampo
Queens Vocational Tech HS	Steve Serber, Gil Rivera
Roosevelt HS (Yonkers)	Jerry Colaio, Dr. Yazullo
Roosevelt HS (Bronx)	Steve Mazzolla, Frank Figarino
Samuel Gompers HS	Elena Papliberios, Ms. Hawthorne, Dennis Abate
Saunders Trades and Tech HS	Bernard P. Pierorazio, Dave Crasson, Joseph Lombardo
Ulster County B.O.C.E.S	Gary Surachi
Van Arsdale HS	Mr. Woodman, Mr. Natal, Mr. Stacy, Mr. Marshal, and Mr. G
William E. Grady VT HS	Tony Valenti, Verna Lauria, Mrs. Paris, Jodi Infantalini
Wingate HS	Herb Hogan
Wings Academy	Mr. Wayne Cox

Appendix V   Prisons where I have presented:
Prisons
Adult Correctional Facility, Rhode Island
Youth Correctional Facility, Rhode Island   John Abate

Dartmouth House of Corrections, MA   Col. Sweeney
Worcester Youth Correctional Facility, MA
Worcester Secure Facility   Tony Nuzzetti, Dawn Perron
Harvard House, MA   J.P. Kalanian
LeeHigh, MA
Norfolk Correctional Facilty, MA

MacDougal Walker Correctional Facility, CT Mr. Smith
Robinson Correctional Facility, CT
Cheshire Correctional Youth Facility, CT

Riker's Island, NY   Frank Dody

A must read!

Author John M. Brucato, a high school principal, has written a useful, easy-to-read book full of practical information while challenging mediocrity.

In Creating a Learning Environment: An Educational Leader's Guide to Managing School Culture, Brucato writes: "Changing the culture of a school or school district is far more difficult than putting together programs and developing policies."

CREATING A
LEARNING
ENVIRONMENT

AN EDUCATIONAL LEADER'S GUIDE TO
MANAGING SCHOOL CULTURE

JOHN M. BRUCATO

He asks many tough and probing questions: Are administrators clear in their expectations of teachers and staff? Are they good role models who gain the trust of all members of the school community through their consistency in dealing with issues? Most importantly, do teachers and staff members like coming to work each day?

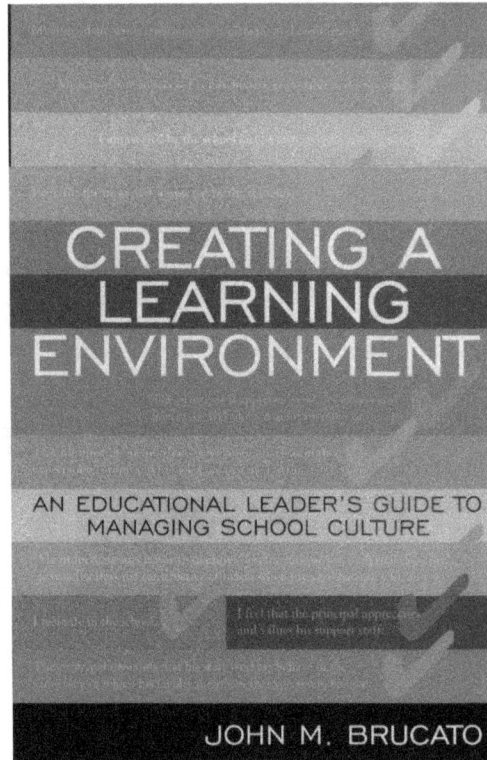

A must read!

James L. Conro's study on best practices used by teachers features real-life classroom examples, do's and don'ts of classroom management, critical components of teaching and learning, and observations of successful teachers in action.

The Faculty Parking Lot Is Not for Planning is an important tool for every new teacher as well as for teacher mentors, department chairs, directors of instruction, and building administrators.

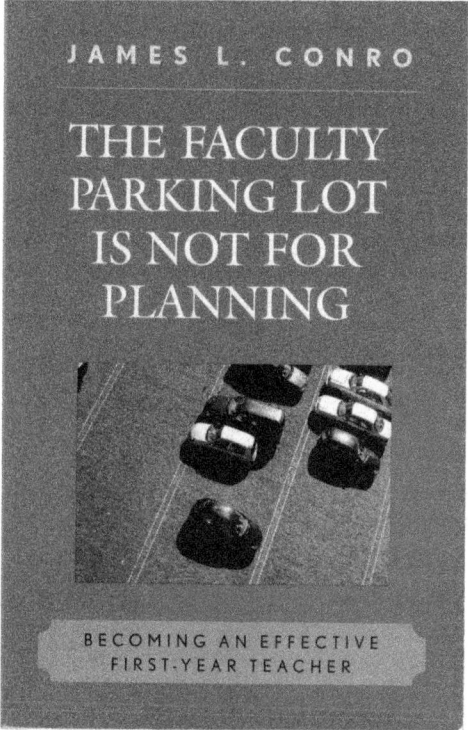

JAMES L. CONRO

THE FACULTY PARKING LOT IS NOT FOR PLANNING

BECOMING AN EFFECTIVE FIRST-YEAR TEACHER

A must read!

In *Reflections of an Urban High School Principal*, Bernard reflects on some of his childhood experiences growing up in the streets of Brooklyn, New York.

He also describes how he survived the New York City public school system as a student, only to return as a teacher, assistant principal, and principal. It is astonishing to read Bernard's revelation that things have not changed in the New York City education system from the time he entered as a kindergarten student some forty years ago.

Reflections of an Urban High School Principal is a must read for educators, students, parents, and any one involved in youth development.

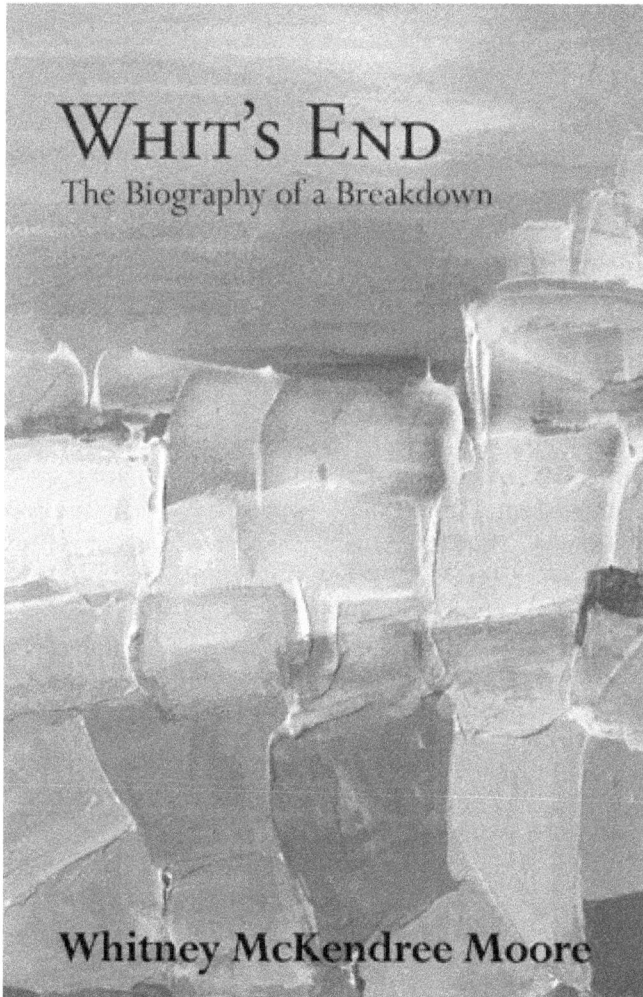

WHIT'S END
The Biography of a Breakdown

Whitney McKendree Moore

"A truly inspirational must read book for those who have the courage to face their weaknessess and pursue their unique greatness."- Mark Mainella

Last Words

The grace of God, a supportive family, and a few loyal friends. They have been the most significant guidance and support in building my career. Having said that, I've got to mention just three names who have gone way beyond in their commitment to putting students first and supporting my efforts in providing timely and thought provoking material.

In Connecticut Rich Cavalaro has gone so far as to email his compatriots, other principals, recommending my programs. He was just transferred from Wilcox to Bullard-Haven, in the hope that he could replicate there what he accomplished at Wilcox. One of the best schools I've ever been in.

In New York, Bernard Gassaway is the personification of a great principal. He's got it all, and he has booked me for years in dozens of schools across the region.

Joe Artuso helps me to be a better human being.

Thank you,

Mark Mainella

www.ingramcontent.com/pod-product-compliance
Lightning Source LLC
Chambersburg PA
CBHW020500030426
42337CB00011B/167